The
Children's
Hymn
Book

The Children's Hymn Book

Compiled and edited by
Kevin Mayhew

Kevin
Mayhew

First published in Great Britain in 1997 by
KEVIN MAYHEW LIMITED
Rattlesden
Bury St Edmunds
Suffolk IP30 0SZ

The following editions are available

Words Only	ISBN	0 86209 942 0
	ISMN	M 57004 012 4
	Catalogue No.	1413051
Full Music (hardback)	ISBN	0 86209 943 9
	ISMN	M 57004 013 1
	Catalogue No.	1413054

Front cover: *Detail of the Angels from the Madonna della Melagrana*
by Sandro Botticelli (1445-1510). Galleria Degli Uffizi,
Florence/Bridgeman Art library, London.
Reproduced by kind permission.

Cover design: Graham Johnstone
Printed and bound in Great Britain

FOREWORD

The Children's Hymn Book presents children with a loving God, involved with and caring for his creation. It promotes positive images of God, the world and humanity, not by denying the reality of negative things in creation, and in ourselves, but by seeing them all in the glorious context of an unconditionally loving God, creator of a fundamentally good world, and humanity made in his image.

The texts chosen evoke images of wonder and hope; they help children feel glad to be alive, angry about injustice, concerned with their environment and, most importantly, to address the question of each individual's relationship with others.

Particular care has been taken to avoid manipulative, archaic and pious language, and hymns of a militaristic or triumphalistic nature have been excluded. Wherever possible, hymns using inclusive language have been preferred and, where language or concepts have changed, texts have been adapted, either to restore the original meaning or to make the general sentiment more appropriate. So, for example, There is a green hill far away now reads 'outside a city wall' rather than 'without'.

The music in *The Children's Hymn Book* is likewise child-centred: tuneful and memorable, gentle and lively. Much thought has been given to the pitch of the tunes and their suitability for young voices.

The keyboard or piano accompaniments have all been specially arranged for the non-specialist player, mostly to a standard of Grade 2. Those with more advanced playing skills will easily fill in with extra notes.

All the songs have elementary guitar chords which may be played with or without a keyboard. On the rare occasions when the two should not be played together I have indicated ✗.

The Children's Hymn Book has been compiled for use in both school and church. It is equally suitable for assembly and for family worship where people of different ages will recognise various layers of meaning in the texts.

For children, as for adults, there is (among many other things) a learning process going on in worship as the faith is expounded, questions are raised and we are encouraged and inspired to deepen our understanding as we open our minds, as well as our hearts, to God in prayer. Any educationalist will confirm that children learn best by participating, and that singing songs is a very important part of that.

I hope that *The Children's Hymn Book* will enable children to participate in worship as fully as they are able; to celebrate the life, love and hope which are at the heart of their enquiring faith; and to grow in that faith and in love of God, each other and themselves.

I am very grateful to those writers, composers and arrangers who have allowed me to use their work in this book, especially Susan Sayers, Michael Forster, Christopher Tambling and Noel Rawsthorne who have each made a major contribution. Norman Vaux has ensured that the guitar chords are playable.

I thank also my colleagues Tracy Cracknell, Nicola Greengrass, Louise Hill, Stephanie Hill, Katherine Laidler, Geoff Peachey, Jane Rayson and Donald Thomson who have worked enthusias- tically and expertly to ensure that *The Children's Hymn Book* is as good as human hands can make it.

KEVIN MAYHEW
Editor

This book is dedicated
to the memory of my father
Walter Mayhew (1907-1996)
who will be enjoying the songs in it,
especially his favourite
'You've gotta move when the Spirit says move'.

1 A butterfly, an Easter egg
Signs of new life

Lively

Leader | *All* | *Leader* | *All* | *Leader*
1. A but-ter-fly, a but-ter-fly, an Eas-ter egg, an Eas-ter egg, a

G | D⁷

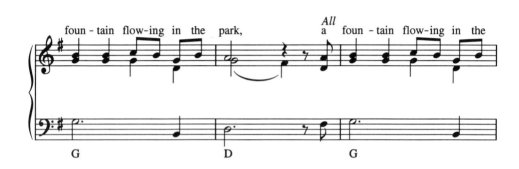

foun - tain flow-ing in the park, *All* a foun - tain flow-ing in the

G | D | G

park. *Refrain* *All* These are signs of new life; the life of Je - sus the

D | G | C | G | D

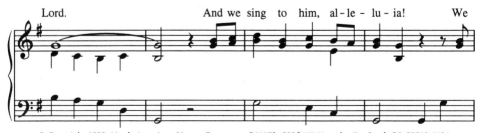

Lord. And we sing to him, al - le - lu - ia! We

2. A helping hand,
   a helping hand,
   a happy smile,
   a happy smile,
   a heart so full of hope and joy,
   a heart so full of hope and joy.

3. A cup of wine,
   a cup of wine,
   a loaf of bread,
   a loaf of bread,
   now blest and broken for us all,
   now blest and broken for us all.

Words: Carey Landry
Music: Carey Landry, arr. Norman Warren

2 A new commandment

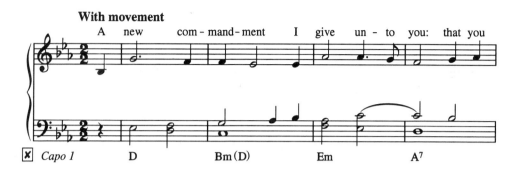

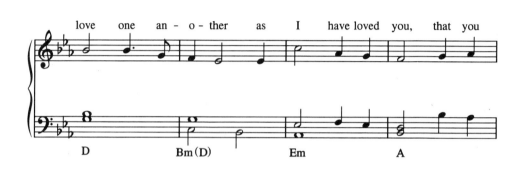

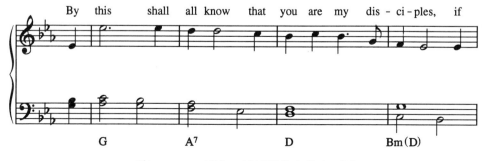

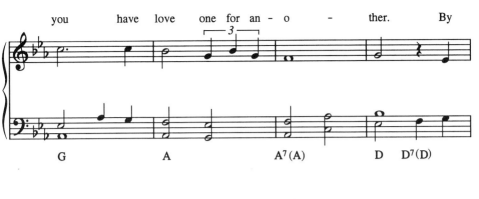

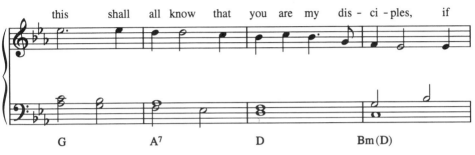

Words: unknown
Music: unknown, arr. Richard Lloyd

3 A still small voice

With an easy swing

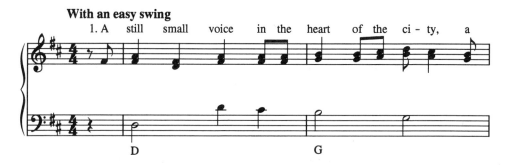

1. A still small voice in the heart of the ci-ty, a

still small voice on the moun-tain, through the storms that are ra-ging or the

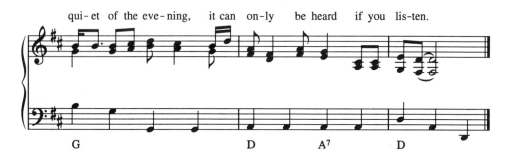

qui-et of the eve-ning, it can on-ly be heard if you lis-ten.

2. The voice of God in a place that is troubled,
   the voice of God in the dawning,
   through the noise of the shouting,
   through the stillness of the sleeping,
   it can only be heard if you listen.

3. Give time to hear, give us love that will listen,
   give wisdom for understanding,
   there's a voice of stillness
   that to each of us is speaking,
   it can only be heard if you listen.

Words: Jancis Harvey
Music: Jancis Harvey, arr. Norman Warren

4 Abba, Father, let me be

Words: Dave Bilbrough
Music: Dave Bilbrough, arr. Christopher Tambling

5 Abba, Father, send your Spirit

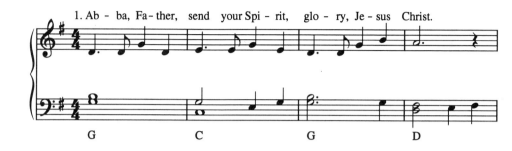

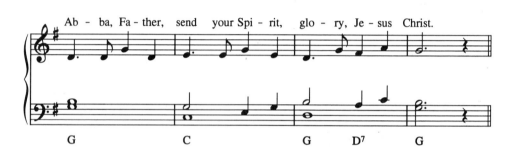

Refrain

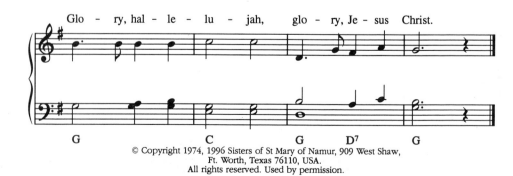

2. If you seek me, you will find me,
   glory, Jesus Christ.
   If you seek me, you will find me,
   glory, Jesus Christ.

3. If you listen, you will hear me,
   glory, Jesus Christ.
   If you listen, you will hear me,
   glory, Jesus Christ.

Words: Rosalie Vissing
Music: Rosalie Vissing, arr. Richard Lloyd

6 All creatures of our God and King

1. All crea-tures of our God and King, lift up your voice and with us

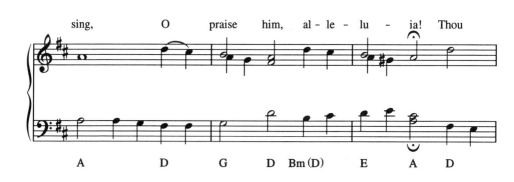

sing, O praise him, al - le - lu - ia! Thou

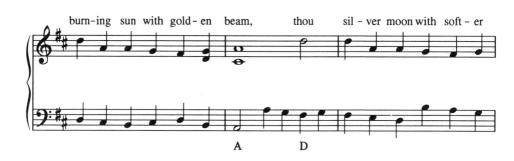

burn-ing sun with gold-en beam, thou sil - ver moon with soft - er

gleam, O praise him, O praise him, al - le -

2. Let all things their Creator bless,
   and worship him in humbleness,
   O praise him, alleluia!
   Praise, praise the Father, praise the Son,
   and praise the Spirit, Three in One.

Words: William Henry Draper, alt.
Music: melody from *Geistliche Kirchengesäng,* arr. Alan Ridout

7 All in an Easter garden

2. All in an Easter garden,
   where water lilies bloom,
   the angels gave their message
   beside an empty tomb:
   'The Lord is here no longer,
   come, see where once he lay;
   the Lord of life is ris'n indeed,
   for this is Easter Day.'

Words: traditional
Music: traditional, arr. Norman Warren

8 All night, all day

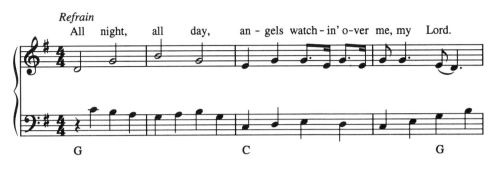

Refrain

All night, all day, an-gels watch-in' o-ver me, my Lord.

G   C   G

All night, all day, an-gels watch-in' o-ver me. *Fine*

D7   G

1. Day is dy-in' in the west, an-gels watch-in' o-ver me, my Lord.

C   G

Sleep, my child, and take your rest, an-gels watch-in' o-ver me. *D.C.*

Em   G   D7   G

2. Now I lay me down to sleep,
    angels watchin' over me, my Lord.
    Pray the Lord my soul to keep,
    angels watchin' over me.

Words: Spiritual
Music: Spiritual, arr. Noel Rawsthorne

9 All of my heart

All of my heart, all of my soul, all of my mind,

Capo 3 D   Em   A   D

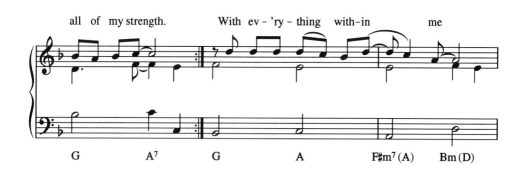

all of my strength. With ev - 'ry - thing with - in me

G   A⁷   G   A   F♯m⁷ (A)   Bm (D)

I want to praise you, Lord.   I want to love you with all

Em   A   D   A   G   A

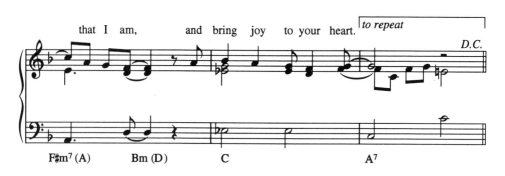

that I am, and bring joy to your heart. *to repeat*

D.C.

F♯m⁷ (A)   Bm (D)   C   A⁷

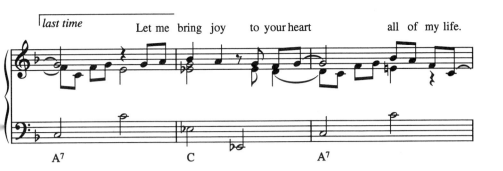

last time

Let me bring joy to your heart all of my life.

A⁷ C A⁷

D Em A D G A⁷ D

Words: Doug Marks-Smirchirch
Music: Doug Marks-Smirchich, arr. Noel Rawsthorne

10 All of the creatures God had made

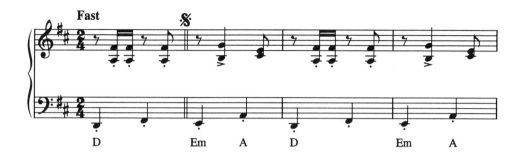

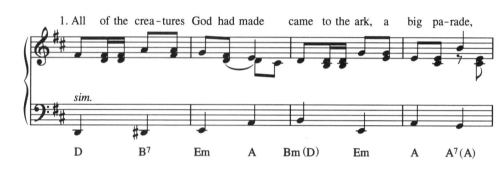

1. All of the crea-tures God had made came to the ark, a big pa-rade,

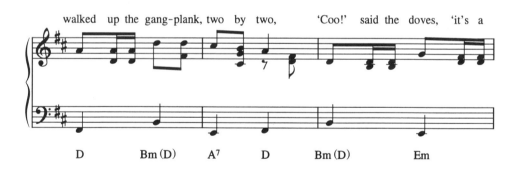

walked up the gang-plank, two by two, 'Coo!' said the doves, 'it's a

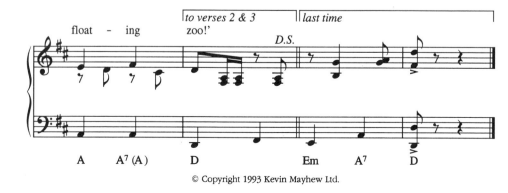

float - ing zoo!'

to verses 2 & 3

last time

2. Ev'rything seemed to come in pairs,
   camels and dogs and big brown bears;
   Noah said to God, 'It's rather rough;
   one of the fleas would be quite enough.'

3. All huddled up in one small space,
   one of the dogs said, 'What a place!
   I haven't room to swing a cat!'
   'Well,' said the cat, 'thank the Lord for that!'

4. People are often like that, too,
   living in boxes, two by two.
   We have to learn to get along,
   just like the animals in this song.

Words: Michael Forster
Music: Christopher Tambling

11 All of the people

you, it's strange, and yet it's true, we start to feel that

Dm   G   C

there is more to life than liv - ing as we

F (Dm)   Dm   C

do. It's rich - er and more sa - tis-fy - ing than we e - ver knew.

D.C.

Dm   G

2. Jesus, Jesus, healing as you go,
   your loving seems to flow
   like water from a fountain,
   and as we are touched we want to grow
   in love towards each other –
   just because you love us so!

3. Jesus, Jesus, we have come to see
   that you must really be
   the Son of God our Father.
   We've been with you and we all agree
   that only in your service
   can the world be truly free!

Words: Susan Sayers
Music: Susan Sayers, arr. Noel Rawsthorne

12 All over the world

2. All over this land the Spirit is moving,
   all over this land,
   as the prophets said it would be.
   All over this land
   there's a mighty revelation
   of the glory of the Lord,
   as the waters cover the sea.

3. All over the Church the Spirit is moving,
   all over the Church,
   as the prophets said it would be.
   All over the Church
   there's a mighty revelation
   of the glory of the Lord,
   as the waters cover the sea.

4. All over us all the Spirit is moving,
   all over us all,
   as the prophets said it would be.
   All over us all
   there's a mighty revelation
   of the glory of the Lord,
   as the waters cover the sea.

5. Deep down in my heart, the Spirit is moving,
   deep down in my heart,
   as the prophets said it would be.
   Deep down in my heart
   there's a mighty revelation
   of the glory of the Lord,
   as the waters cover the sea.

Words: Roy Turner
Music: Roy Turner, arr. Noel Rawsthorne

13 All that I am

1. All that I am, all that I do,

all that I'll e-ver have I of-fer now to you.

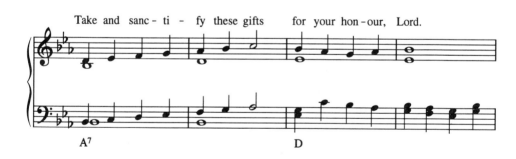

Take and sanc-ti-fy these gifts for your hon-our, Lord.

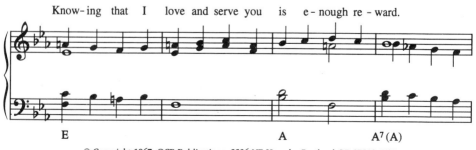

Know-ing that I love and serve you is e-nough re-ward.

All that I am, all that I do,

D   A⁷   D

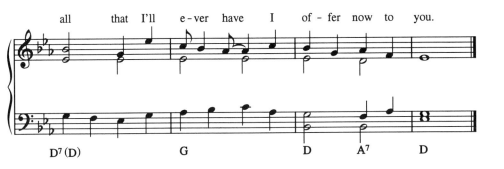

all that I'll e-ver have I of – fer now to you.

D⁷ (D)   G   D   A⁷   D

2. All that I dream, all that I pray,
   all that I'll ever make I give to you today.
   Take and sanctify these gifts
   for your honour, Lord.
   Knowing that I love and serve you
   is enough reward.
   All that I am, all that I do,
   all that I'll ever have I offer now to you.

Words: Sebastian Temple
Music: Sebastian Temple, arr. Noel Rawsthorne

14 All the nations of the earth

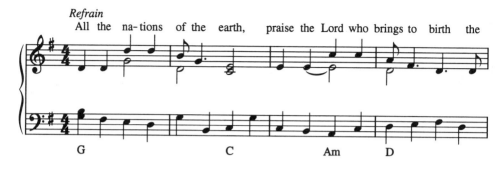

Refrain

All the na-tions of the earth, praise the Lord who brings to birth the

G   C   Am   D

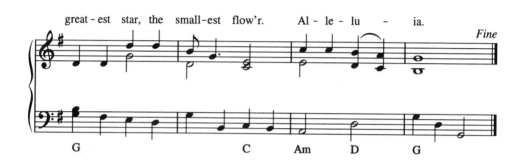

great - est star, the small-est flow'r. Al - le - lu - ia.   *Fine*

G   C   Am   D   G

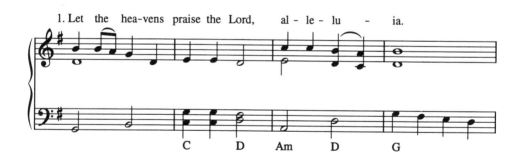

1. Let the hea-vens praise the Lord, al - le - lu - ia.

C   D   Am   D   G

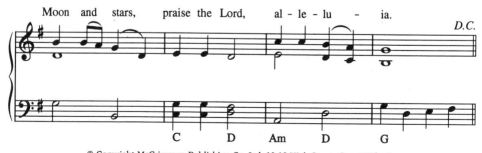

Moon and stars, praise the Lord, al - le - lu - ia.   *D.C.*

C   D   Am   D   G

2. Snow-capped mountains, praise the Lord,
   alleluia.
   Rolling hills, praise the Lord,
   alleluia.

3. Deep sea water, praise the Lord,
   alleluia.
   Gentle rain, praise the Lord,
   alleluia.

4. Roaring lion, praise the Lord,
   alleluia.
   Singing birds, praise the Lord,
   alleluia.

5. Earthly monarchs, praise the Lord,
   alleluia.
   Young and old, praise the Lord,
   alleluia.

Words: Michael Cockett
Music: Kevin Mayhew, arr. Noel Rawsthorne

15 All things bright and beautiful (Tune 1)

Refrain

All things bright and beau - ti - ful, all crea - tures great and small,

all things wise and won - der - ful, the Lord God made them all. *Fine*

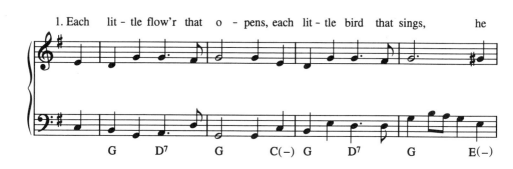

1. Each lit - tle flow'r that o - pens, each lit - tle bird that sings, he

made their glow- ing col - ours, he made their ti - ny wings. *D.C.*

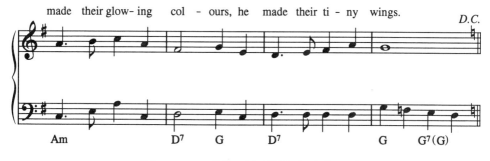

This arrangement © Copyright 1994 Kevin Mayhew Ltd.

2. The purple-headed mountain,
   the river running by,
   the sunset and the morning
   that brightens up the sky.

3. The cold wind in the winter,
   the pleasant summer sun,
   the ripe fruits in the garden,
   he made them ev'ry one.

4. He gave us eyes to see them,
   and lips that we might tell
   how great is God almighty
   who has made all things well.

Words: Cecil Frances Alexander
Music: traditional English melody, arr. Alan Ridout

15a All things bright and beautiful (Tune 2)

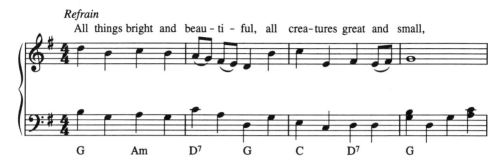

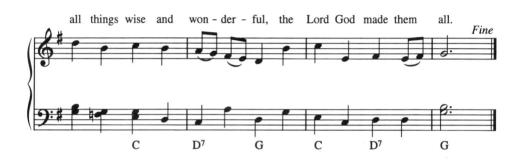

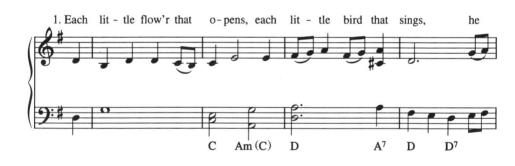

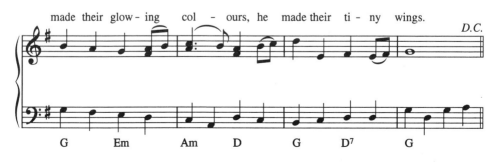

2. The purple-headed mountain,
   the river running by,
   the sunset and the morning
   that brightens up the sky.

3. The cold wind in the winter,
   the pleasant summer sun,
   the ripe fruits in the garden,
   he made them ev'ry one.

4. He gave us eyes to see them,
   and lips that we might tell
   how great is God almighty
   who has made all things well.

Words: Cecil Frances Alexander
Music: traditional English melody, arr. Alan Ridout

The
Children's
Hymn
Book

16 Alleluia, alleluia, give thanks to the risen Lord

Refrain

Al-le-lu-ia, al-le-lu-ia, give thanks to the ri-sen Lord, al-le-

Capo 3   D   Bm(D)   Em   A⁷

lu-ia, al-le-lu-ia, give praise to his name. *Fine*

D   Bm(D)   A⁷   D

1. Je-sus is Lord of all the earth,

Bm(D)   G   A

he is the King of cre-a - tion. *D.C.*

D   Bm(D)   G   A⁷

2. Spread the good news o'er all the earth,
   Jesus has died and has risen.

3. Come, let us praise the living God,
   joyfully sing to our Saviour.

Words: Donald Fishel
Music: Donald Fishel, arr. Alan Ridout

17 And everyone beneath the vine and fig tree
The vine and fig tree

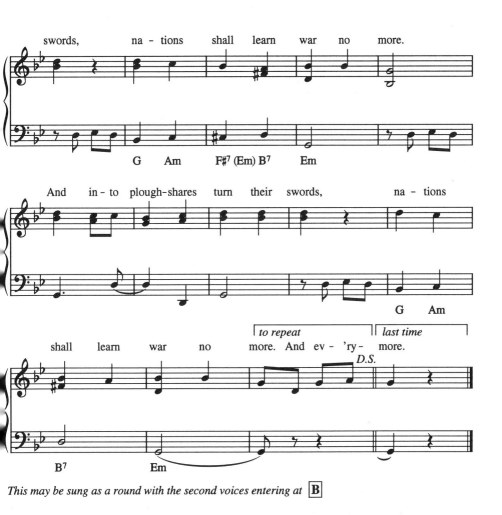

This may be sung as a round with the second voices entering at **B**

Words: unknown
Music: unknown, arr. Noel Rawsthorne

18 Anytime, anywhere
My best friend

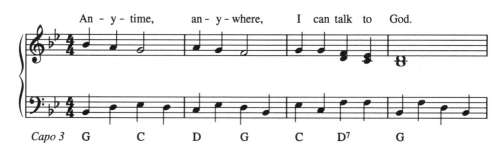

An - y - time, an - y - where, I can talk to God.

Capo 3 G   C   D   G   C   D⁷   G

When I'm glad, when I'm sad, I can talk to God.

D   D⁷(D)   G   D   A⁷   D   D⁷(D)

Some-times on my knees I pray, some-times as I work or play,

G   C   A⁷   D⁷

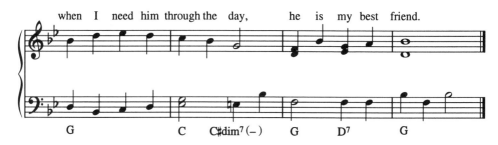

when I need him through the day, he is my best friend.

G   C   C♯dim⁷(−)   G   D⁷   G

Words: Barbara Ryberg
Music: Ruth Brabazon, arr. Noel Rawsthorne

19 Be still and know

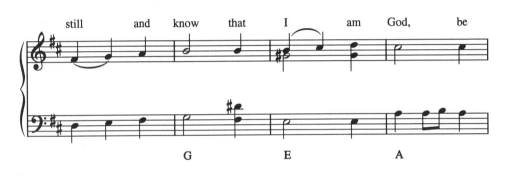

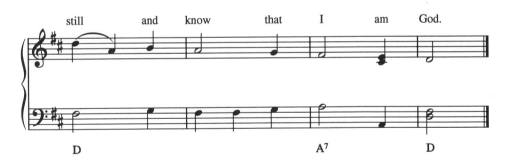

2. In you, O Lord, I put my trust,
    in you, O Lord, I put my trust,
    in you, O Lord, I put my trust.

Words: unknown, based on Psalm 46
Music: unknown, arr. Alan Ridout

20 Be still, for the presence of the Lord

Reverently

2. Be still, for the glory of the Lord is shining all around;
   he burns with holy fire, with splendour he is crowned.
   How awesome is the sight, our radiant King of light!
   Be still, for the glory of the Lord is shining all around.

3. Be still, for the power of the Lord is moving in this place;
   he comes to cleanse and heal, to minister his grace.
   No work too hard for him, in faith receive from him.
   Be still, for the power of the Lord is moving in this place.

Words: David J. Evans
Music: David J. Evans, arr. Christopher Tambling

21 Be the centre of my life

Gently

1. Be the cen-tre of my life, Lord Je-sus, be the

C

cen-tre of my life, I pray; be my Sa-viour to for-give me, be my

G   F (Dm)

friend to be with me, be the cen-tre of my life to-day!

C   G   C

2. Let the power of your presence, Lord Jesus,
   from the centre of my life shine through;
   oh, let ev'rybody know it,
   I really want to show it,
   that the centre of my life is you!

Words: Alan J. Price
Music: Alan J. Price, arr. Norman Warren

22 Bind us together, Lord

Steadily, not too fast

Refrain

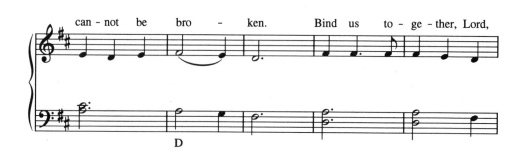

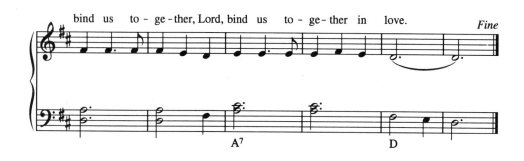

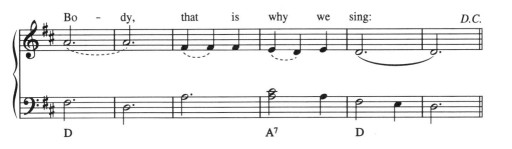

2. Fit for the glory of God,
   purchased by his precious Blood,
   born with the right to be free:
   Jesus the vict'ry has won.

3. We are the fam'ly of God,
   we are his promise divine,
   we are his chosen desire,
   we are the glorious new wine.

Words: Bob Gillman
Music: Bob Gillman, arr. Alan Ridout

23 Bless the Lord, O my soul

Words: from Psalm 103:1
Music: unknown, arr. John Ballantine

24 Blest are you, Lord, God of all creation

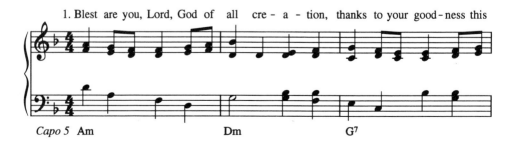

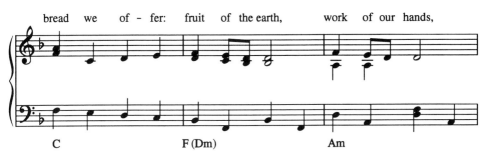

bread we of - fer: fruit of the earth, work of our hands,

C   F (Dm)   Am

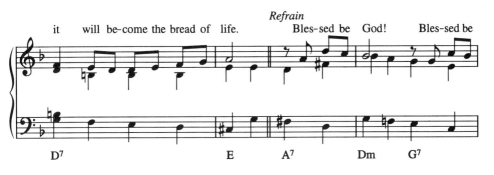

it will be-come the bread of life.   *Refrain*   Bles-sed be God!   Bles-sed be

D⁷   E   A⁷   Dm   G⁷

God!   Bles-sed be God for e - ver!   A - men!   Bles-sed be

C   F (Dm)   Dm   E   Am   A⁷

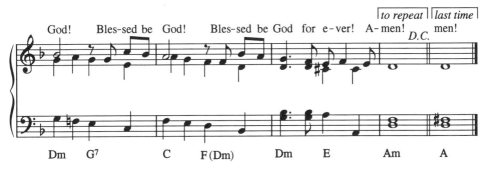

to repeat *last time*

God!   Bles-sed be God!   Bles-sed be God for e-ver!   A-men!   men!
D.C.

Dm   G⁷   C   F (Dm)   Dm   E   Am   A

2   Blest are you, Lord, God of all creation,
thanks to your goodness this wine we offer:
fruit of the earth, work of our hands,
it will become the cup of life.

Words: Aniceto Nazareth
Music: Aniceto Nazareth, arr. Noel Rawsthorne

25 Boisterous, buzzing, barking things
Big and little you's and me's

Whimsical

1. Bois-t'rous, buz-zing, bark-ing things, with paws and legs and claws and wings; all that swims or crawls or sings; or flaps or flops or flips or flings: our Cre-a-tor made all these, and big and lit-tle you's and me's.

to verses 2 & 3

last time

big and lit-tle you's and me's.

2. Bugs and birds and bears and bees;
   and buds that burst on blossoming trees;
   fluffy clouds before the breeze;
   and stars and skies and streams and seas:
   our Creator made all these,
   and big and little you's and me's.

3. Girls and boys and Mum and Dad,
   the kind and good, or even bad –
   all who please and make him glad,
   and even those who make him sad:
   our Creator made all these,
   and big and little you's and me's.

Words: Winifred Elliott
Music: Winifred Elliott, arr. Noel Rawsthorne

26 Break the bread and pour the wine

Smoothly

Refrain

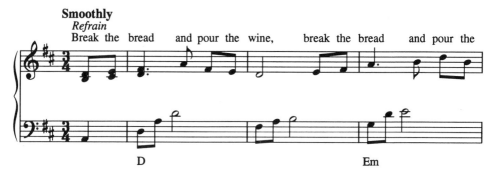

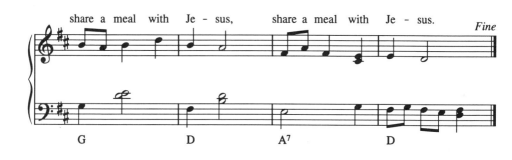

we can share with one a - no - ther   ev - 'ry-thing we have that's good.

D.C.

E   A   E   A

2. Come and meet around the table,
   God provides the wine to share;
   we enjoy a meal together,
   show each other how we care.

Words: Michael Forster
Music: Christopher Tambling

27 Brother, sister, let me serve you

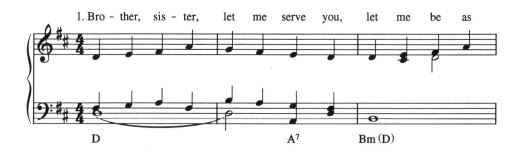

1. Bro-ther, sis-ter, let me serve you, let me be as

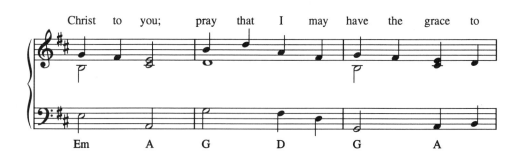

Christ to you; pray that I may have the grace to

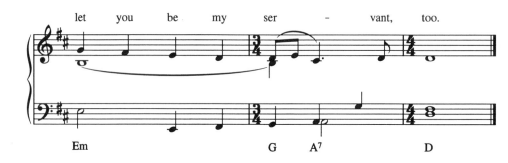

let you be my ser - vant, too.

2. We are pilgrims on a journey,
fellow trav'lers on the road;
we are here to help each other
walk the mile and bear the load.

3. I will hold the Christlight for you
in the night-time of your fear;
I will hold my hand out to you,
speak the peace you long to hear.

4. I will weep when you are weeping;
   when you laugh, I'll laugh with you.
   I will share your joy and sorrow,
   till we've seen this journey through.

5. When we sing to God in heaven,
   we shall find such harmony,
   born of all we've known together
   of Christ's love and agony.

6. Brother, sister, let me serve you,
   let me be as Christ to you;
   pray that I may have the grace to
   let you be my servant, too.

Words: Richard Gillard
Music: Richard Gillard, arr. Richard Lloyd

28 Caterpillar, caterpillar

1. Cat- er- pil - lar, cat- er- pil - lar, munch - ing, munch - ing, ate through a leaf or two, for cat- er- pil - lar, cat- er- pil - lar, munch - ing, munch - ing, did-n't have a lot to do.

But the leaves were ve - ry ta - sty, and there seemed a lot to spare, so cat- er- pil - lar, cat- er- pil - lar

last time go to ⊕

went on munch - ing, munch - ing ev- 'ry - where. *D.C.*

Am   Dm   E   Am

⊕ CODA

me;   for he took me as a cat - er -

E   Am   Em   Am

rit.   *much slower*

pil - lar, and he made a but - ter - fly of me.'

Dm   E   F(Dm)   Dm   E   Am

2. Caterpillar, caterpillar, feeling sleepy,
   fixed up a silken bed.
   Then caterpillar, caterpillar climbed inside
   and covered up his sleepy head.
   In the dark he slept and rested
   as the days and nights went by,
   till on a sunny morning when the silk bed burst,
   he was a butterfly!

3. Butterfly, oh butterfly, a-flitt'ring, flutt'ring;
   oh what a sight to see.
   And as the lovely butterfly was flutt'ring by,
   I heard him sing a song to me:
   'Oh I never knew God could do
   such a wondrous thing for me;
   for he took me as a caterpillar and he made
   a butterfly of me.'

Words: Susan Sayers
Music: Susan Sayers, arr. Noel Rawsthorne

29 Change my heart, O God

Words: Eddie Espinosa
Music: Eddie Espinosa, arr. Christopher Tambling

30 'Cheep!' said the sparrow
The birds' song

2. 'Coo!' said the gentle one, the grey-blue dove,
   'I can tell you that God is love.'
   High up above sang the lark in flight,
   'I know the Lord is my heart's delight.'

3. 'Chirp!' said the robin with his breast so red,
   'I don't work at all, yet I'm fed.'
   'Whoo!' called the owl in a leafy wood.
   'Our God is wonderful, wise and good.'

Words: Estelle White
Music: Estelle White, arr. Noel Rawsthorne

31 Clap your hands, all you people

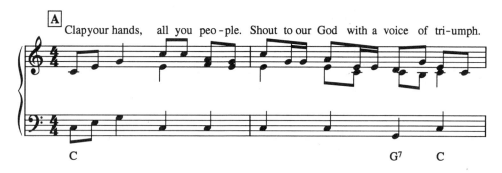

This may be sung as a round with the second voices entering at B

Words: Jimmy Owens
Music: Jimmy Owens, arr. Noel Rawsthorne

32 Clap your hands and sing this song

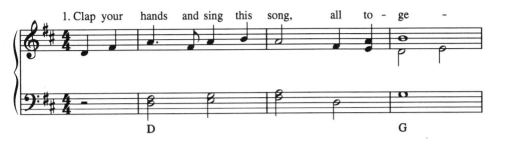

2. Raise your hands up in the air, all together,
   God can reach you anywhere, all together.

3. Fold your arms across your chest, all together,
   in the arms of God you're blessed, all together.

4. Close your eyes and shut them tight, all together,
   God will keep you in his sight, all together.

5. Now sing softly, whisper low, all together,
   God will hear you even so, all together.

6. Sing out loud and strong and clear, all together,
   so that ev'ryone can hear, all together.

7. Sing with harmony and joy, all together,
   God loves ev'ry girl and boy, all together.

Words: Jean Holloway
Music: traditional, arr. Richard Lloyd

33 Colours of day
Light up the fire

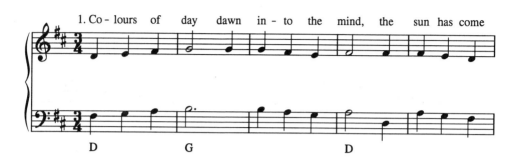

1. Co-lours of day dawn in-to the mind, the sun has come

D   G   D

up, the night is be-hind. Go down in the ci-ty, in-to the

A⁷   D   G

street, and let's give the mes-sage to the peo-ple we meet.

D   A⁷   D

Refrain

So light up the fire and let the flame burn, o-pen the

D⁷   G   D

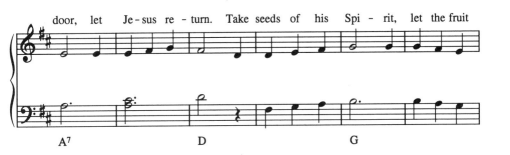

door, let Je-sus re - turn. Take seeds of his Spi - rit, let the fruit

A⁷ D G

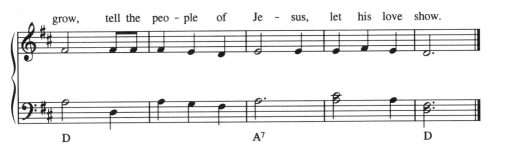

grow, tell the peo - ple of Je - sus, let his love show.

D A⁷ D

2. Go through the park, on into the town;
   the sun still shines on, it never goes down.
   The light of the world is risen again;
   the people of darkness are needing a friend.

3. Open your eyes, look into the sky,
   the darkness has come, the sun came to die.
   The evening draws on, the sun disappears,
   but Jesus is living, his Spirit is near.

Words: Sue McClellan, John Paculabo and Keith Ryecroft
Music: Sue McClellan, John Paculabo and Keith Ryecroft, arr. Alan Ridout

The
Children's
Hymn
Book

34 Come into his presence

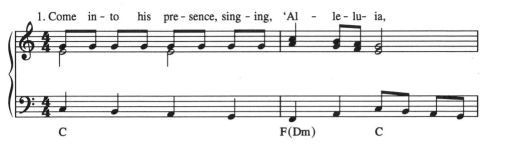

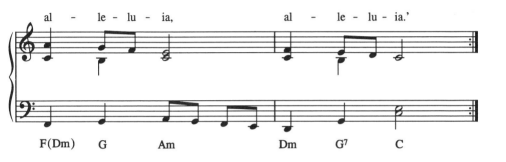

2. Come into his presence, singing,
   'Jesus is Lord, Jesus is Lord, Jesus is Lord.'
   Come into his presence, singing,
   'Jesus is Lord, Jesus is Lord, Jesus is Lord.'

3. Come into his presence, singing,
   'Glory to God, glory to God, glory to God.'
   Come into his presence, singing,
   'Glory to God, glory to God, glory to God.'

Words: unknown
Music: unknown, arr. Noel Rawsthorne

35 Come on and celebrate
Celebrate

Very lively

Come on and ce-le-brate! His gift of love we will

ce-le-brate — the Son of God who loved us

and gave us life. We'll shout your praise, O King:

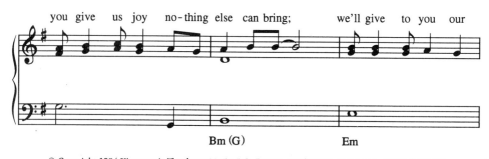

you give us joy no-thing else can bring; we'll give to you our

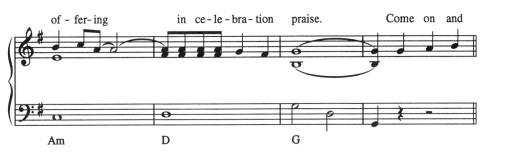

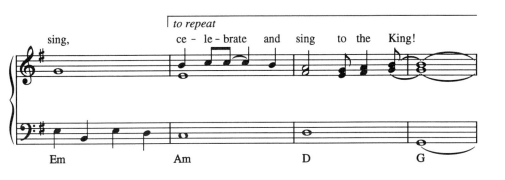

Words: Patricia Morgan
Music: Patricia Morgan, arr. Christopher Tambling

36 Come on, let's get up and go

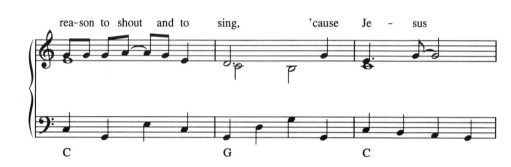

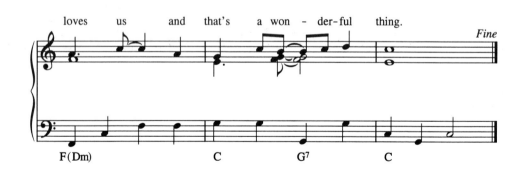

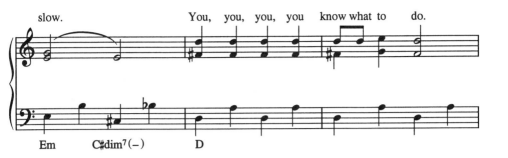

slow. You, you, you, you know what to do.

Em   C#dim⁷(−)   D

Give your life to him. Come on, let's

G   D   G   D   G⁷

D.S.

Words: Graham Kendrick
Music: Graham Kendrick, arr. Noel Rawsthorne

37 Do not be afraid

Refrain

Do not be a-fraid, for I have re-deemed you.

Capo 3   D   Em   A⁷   D

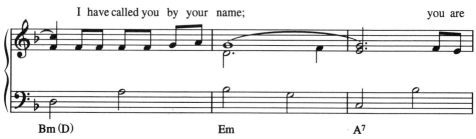

I have called you by your name; you are

Bm (D)   Em   A⁷

mine.   *Fine*   1. When you walk through the wa-ters I'll be

D   G   D   Bm (D)   G

with you.   You will ne-ver sink be-neath the waves.   *D.C.*

A   G   A   D

2. When the fear of loneliness is looming,
   then remember I am at your side.

3. You are mine, O my child, I am your Father,
   and I love you with a perfect love.

Words: Gerard Markland
Music: Gerard Markland, arr. Noel Rawsthorne

38 Do what you know is right

Brightly

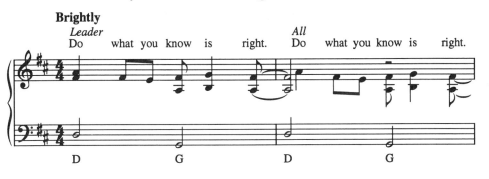

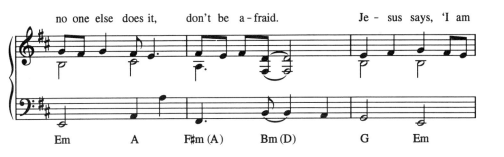

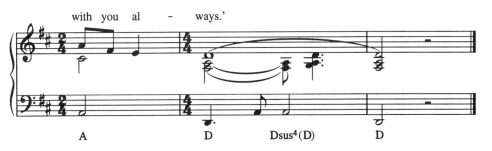

Words: Bev Gammon
Music: Bev Gammon, arr. Noel Rawsthorne

39 Do you ever wish you could fly
Just be glad God made you 'you'

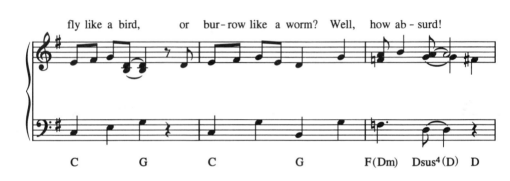

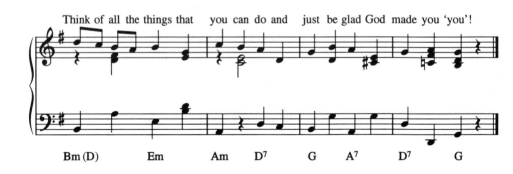

2. Do you ever wish you could swim like a duck?
Unless your feet are webbed you're out of luck!
Think of all the things that you can do
and just be glad God made you 'you'!

3. Do you ever wish you could run like a hare?
   Well, wishing it won't get you anywhere!
   Think of all the things that you can do
   and just be glad God made you 'you'!

4. Do you ever wish you could hang like a bat?
   There's really not a lot of fun in that!
   Think of all the things that you can do
   and just be glad God made you 'you'!

5. Do you ever wish – well, that's really enough!
   To wish away your life is silly stuff!
   Think of all the things that you can do
   and just be glad God made you 'you'!

Words: Michael Forster
Music: Christopher Tambling

40 Don't build your house on the sandy land
Sandy land

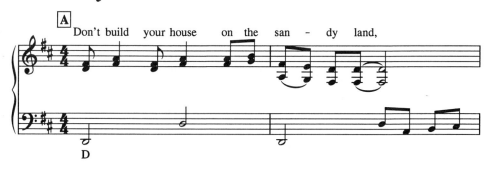

Don't build your house on the san - dy land,

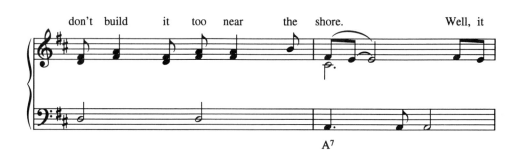

don't build it too near the shore. Well, it

might look kind of nice, but you'll have to build it twice, oh, you'll

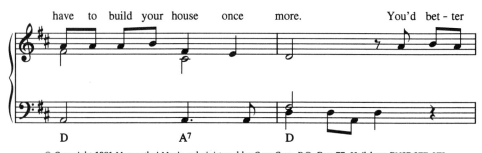

have to build your house once more. You'd bet - ter

This song may be sung as a round with the second voices entering at B

Words: Karen Lafferty
Music: Karen Lafferty, arr. Noel Rawsthorne

41 Each of us is a living stone
Living stones

Brightly (swinging)
Refrain

Each of us is a liv-ing stone   no one needs to stand a - lone,

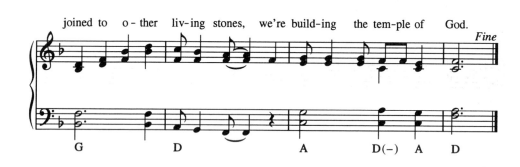

Capo 3   D   A⁷   D

joined to o - ther liv-ing stones, we're build-ing   the tem-ple of   God.
Fine

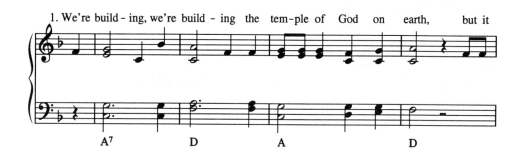

G   D   A   D(−)   A   D

1. We're build - ing, we're build - ing the tem-ple of God on earth, but it

A⁷   D   A   D

needs no walls or stee - ple, for we're ma - king a house of grea-ter worth, we're

A⁷   D   A⁷   D

2. The stone that, the stone that the builders once cast aside
   has been made the firm foundation,
   and the carpenter who was crucified
   now offers us salvation.

Words: Michael Forster
Music: James Patten

42 Enter the darkness

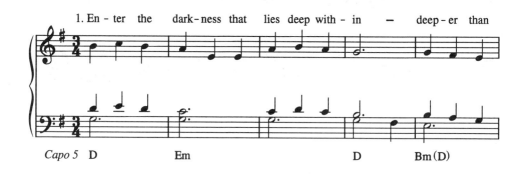

1. En-ter the dark-ness that lies deep with-in — deep-er than

Capo 5 D   Em   D   Bm(D)

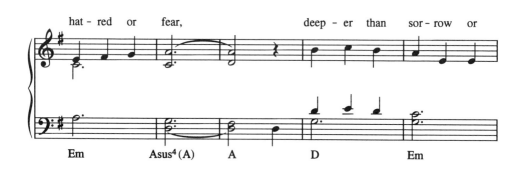

hat-red or fear, deep-er than sor-row or

Em   Asus⁴(A)   A   D   Em

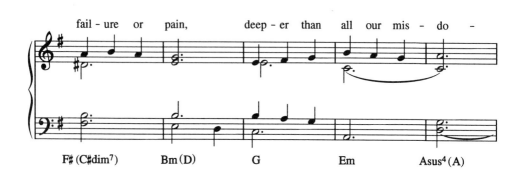

fail-ure or pain, deep-er than all our mis-do-

F#(C#dim⁷)   Bm(D)   G   Em   Asus⁴(A)

ings. Trust the my-st'ry, trust its

A   C   Dm   E

love and wis - dom, trust and rev - 'rence

Am   D   Bm (D)   F#m (A)

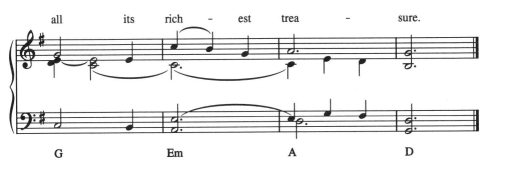

all its rich - est trea - sure.

G   Em   A   D

2. Enter the stillness and find your true peace –
   enter the oneness of life.
   God is the darkness and God is the peace,
   God is the stillness of healing.
   God is oneness, source of bliss and wonder,
   God is myst'ry, love that knows no measure.

Words: W.L. Wallace
Music: Richard Lloyd

43 Every minute of every day

Driving beat

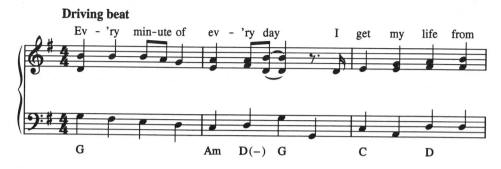

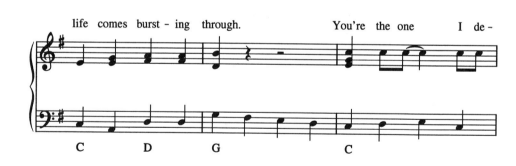

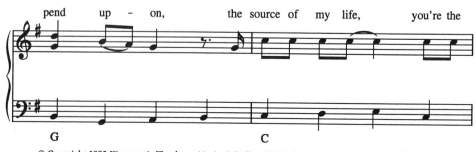

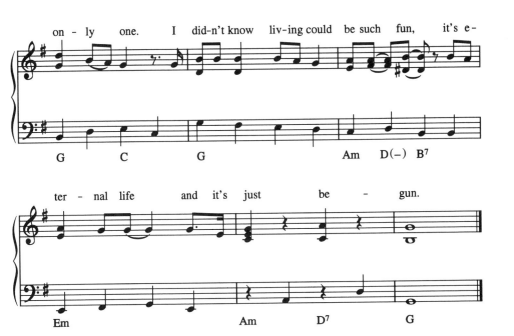

Words: Stuart Garrard
Music: Stuart Garrard, arr. Noel Rawsthorne

44 Father, I place into your hands

Gently

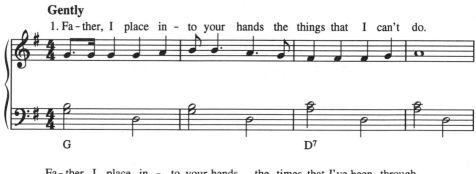

1. Fa-ther, I place in-to your hands the things that I can't do.

G   D⁷

Fa-ther, I place in-to your hands the times that I've been through.

G

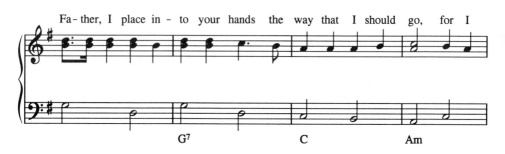

Fa-ther, I place in-to your hands the way that I should go, for I

G⁷   C   Am

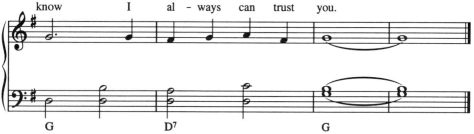

know   I   al-ways   can   trust   you.

G   D⁷   G

2. Father, I place into your hands
   my friends and family.
   Father, I place into your hands
   the things that trouble me.
   Father, I place into your hands
   the person I would be,
   for I know I always can trust you.

3. Father, we love to seek your face,
   we love to hear your voice.
   Father, we love to sing your praise,
   and in your name rejoice.
   Father, we love to walk with you,
   and in your presence rest,
   for we know we always can trust you.

4. Father, I want to be with you
   and do the things you do.
   Father, I want to speak the words
   that you are speaking too.
   Father, I want to love the ones
   that you will draw to you,
   for I know that I am one with you.

Words: Jenny Hewer
Music: Jenny Hewer, arr. Christopher Tambling

45 Father, we adore you

Worshipfully

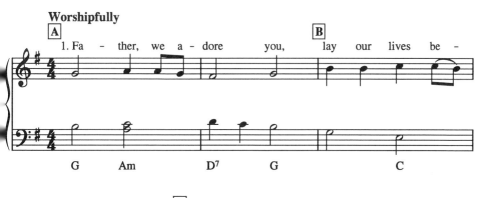

1. Father, we adore you, lay our lives be-fore you.

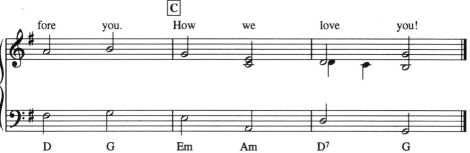

fore you. How we love you!

This may be sung as a round with entries at A, B *and* C

2. Jesus, we adore you,
   lay our lives before you.
   How we love you!

3. Spirit, we adore you,
   lay our lives before you.
   How we love you!

Words: Terrye Coelho
Music: Terrye Coelho, arr. Christopher Tambling

46 Father, we love you
Glorify your name

Worshipfully

1. Fa - ther, we love you, we praise you, we a - dore you,

C   F (Dm)   G⁷   C

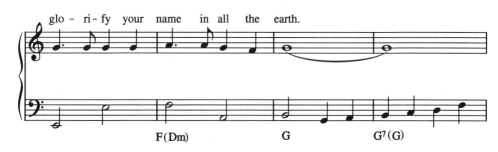

glo - ri - fy your name in all the earth.

F (Dm)   G   G⁷ (G)

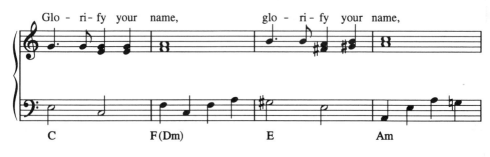

Glo - ri - fy your name, glo - ri - fy your name,

C   F (Dm)   E   Am

glo - ri - fy your name in all the earth.

F (Dm)   G⁷   C

2. Jesus, we love you,
    we praise you, we adore you,
    glorify your name in all the earth.
    Glorify your name, glorify your name,
    glorify your name in all the earth.

3. Spirit, we love you,
    we praise you, we adore you,
    glorify your name in all the earth.
    Glorify your name, glorify your name,
    glorify your name in all the earth.

Words: Donna Adkins
Music: Donna Adkins, arr. Christopher Tambling

47 Father, we want to thank you

Refrain

Father, we want to thank you for your loving kindness; and to show you we love you we will play our music for you.

Capo 3 D   Em   D

Bm (D)   Em   A⁷   D

1. Rum, tum, ta-rum, tum, tum, we play our drums for you, Lord Jesus.

A   D   Em   A   D

Rum, tum, ta-rum, tum, tum, we play our drums for you.

A   D   Em   A   D

2. Ring, ting, ta-ting, ting, ting,
   we play our triangles for Jesus.
   Ring, ting, ta-ting, ting, ting,
   we play them, Lord, for you.

3. La, la, la-la, la, la,
   we sing our praises for you, Jesus.
   La, la, la-la, la, la,
   we sing our praise for you.

Words: Susan Sayers
Music: Susan Sayers, arr. Noel Rawsthorne

48 Father welcomes all his children

Refrain

Fa - ther wel - comes all his chil - dren to his fam - 'ly through his Son.

Capo 3   D   A   Bm (D)   F#m (A)   G   D

through his Son. Fa - ther giv - ing his sal - va - tion,

Em   A   D   A   Bm (D)   F#m (A)

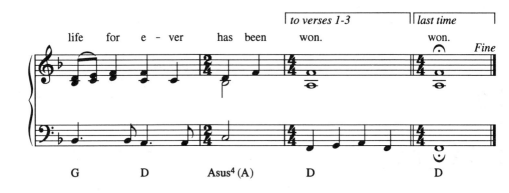

life for e - ver has been won. won. *Fine*

to verses 1-3   *last time*

G   D   Asus⁴ (A)   D   D

1. Lit - tle chil - dren, come to me, for my king - dom is of these.

F#m (A)   Bm (D)   Em   Bm (D) F#m (A)   Bm (D)   Em   A

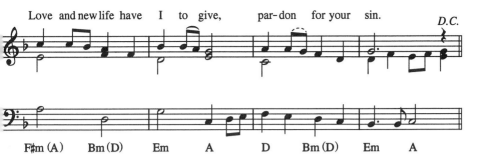

Love and new life have I to give, par-don for your sin.

D.C.

F#m (A)   Bm (D)   Em   A   D   Bm (D)   Em   A

2. In the water, in the word,
   in his promise, be assured:
   all who believe and are baptised
   shall be born again.

3. Let us daily die to sin;
   let us daily rise with him –
   walk in the love of Christ our Lord,
   live in the peace of God.

Words: Robin Mann
Music: Robin Mann, arr. Noel Rawsthorne

The
Children's
Hymn
Book

49 Fishes of the ocean

1. Fish-es of the o-cean and the birds of the air, they all de-
clare the won-der-ful works of God who has cre - a - ted ev - 'ry-
thing ev -'ry-where; let the whole earth sing of his love!

C | F (Dm) | Am | F (Dm)
C | G | C | F (Dm)
C | G | C

2. Apples in the orchard and the corn in the field,
   the plants all yield their fruit in due season,
   so the generosity of God is revealed;
   let the whole earth sing of his love!

3. Energy and colour from the sun with its light,
   the moon by night; the patterns of stars
   all winking in the darkness on a frosty cold night;
   let the whole earth sing of his love!

4. Muddy hippopotamus and dainty gazelle,
   the mice as well, are all of his making,
   furry ones and hairy ones and some with a shell;
   let the whole earth sing of his love!

5. All that we can hear and ev'rything we can see,
   including me, we all of us spring from God
   who cares for ev'rybody unendingly;
   let the whole earth sing of his love!

Words: Susan Sayers
Music: Susan Sayers, arr. Noel Rawsthorne

50 Follow me

Refrain
Fol - low me, fol-low me, leave your home and fa - mi -
ly, leave your fish-ing nets and boats up-on the shore.
Leave the seeds that you have sown, leave the crops that you've
grown, leave the peo-ple you have known and fol-low me.
1. The fox - es have their holes and the swal-lows have their

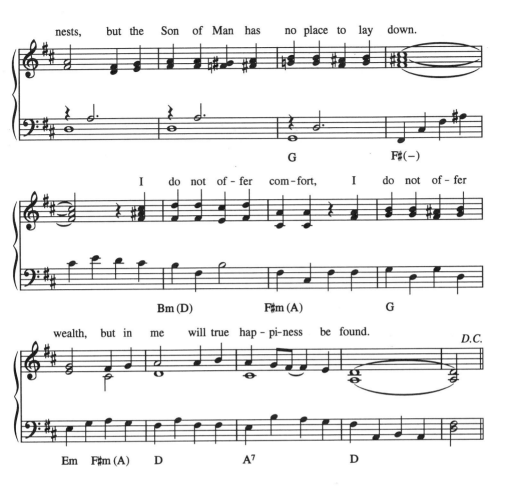

nests, but the Son of Man has no place to lay down.

G *F♯(−)*

I do not of-fer com-fort, I do not of-fer

Bm (D) *F♯m (A)* *G*

wealth, but in me will true hap-pi-ness be found.

D.C.

Em F♯m (A) *D* *A⁷* *D*

2. If you would follow me,
   you must leave old ways behind.
   You must take my cross
   and follow on my path.
   You may be far from loved ones,
   you may be far from home,
   but my Father will welcome you at last.

3. Although I go away
   you will never be alone,
   for the Spirit will be there
   to comfort you.
   Though all of you may scatter,
   each follow their own path,
   still the Spirit of love will lead you home.

Words: Michael Cockett
Music: Sister Madeleine, arr. Noel Rawsthorne

51 Friends, all gather here in a circle
Circle of friends

Friends, all ga-ther here in a cir-cle. It has no be-gin-ning and it

C   F(Dm)   C   F(Dm)   C   Dm

has no end. Face to face, we all have a place in

G   C   F(Dm)   C   F(Dm)

God's own cir-cle of friends. Hey there, *(name)*! How do you do?

C   G⁷   C   F(Dm)   C   G

Who's that friend sit-ting close to you? Thank the Lord, for

C   Am   Dm   G⁷   C   Dm

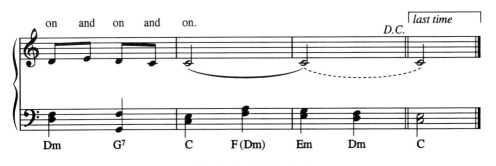

Words: David Morstad
Music: David Morstad, arr. Noel Rawsthorne

52 From heaven you came
The Servant King

Worshipfully

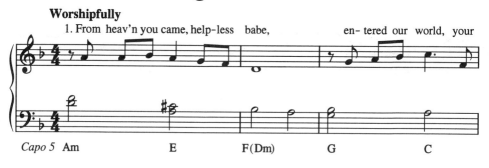

1. From heav'n you came, help-less babe, en-tered our world, your

Capo 5 Am   E   F(Dm)   G   C

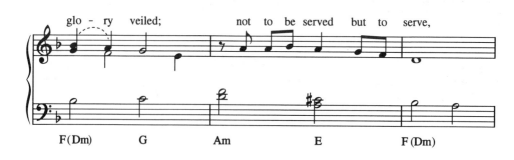

glo – ry veiled; not to be served but to serve,

F(Dm)   G   Am   E   F(Dm)

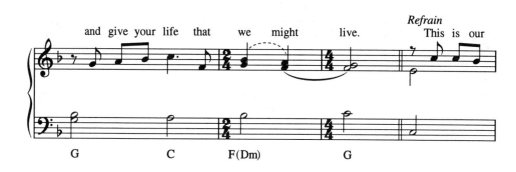

and give your life that we might live. *Refrain* This is our

G   C   F(Dm)   G

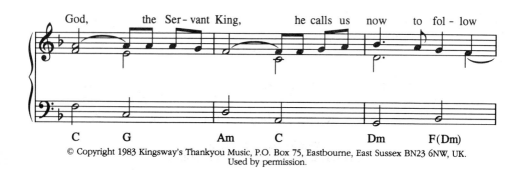

God, the Ser-vant King, he calls us now to fol-low

C   G   Am   C   Dm   F(Dm)

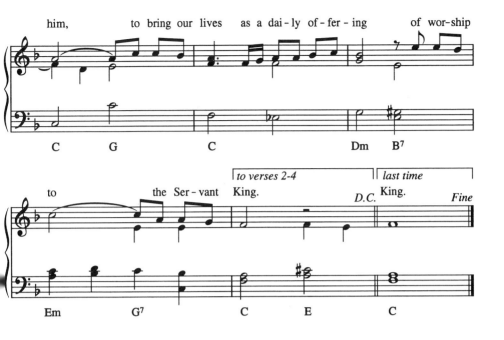

2. There in the garden of tears,
   my heavy load he chose to bear;
   his heart with sorrow was torn,
   'Yet not my will, but yours,' he said.

3. Come, see his hands and his feet,
   the scars that speak of sacrifice,
   hands that flung stars into space
   to cruel nails surrendered.

4. So let us learn how to serve,
   and in our lives enthrone him;
   each other's needs to prefer,
   for it is Christ we're serving.

Words: Graham Kendrick
Music: Graham Kendrick, arr. Christopher Tambling

53 From my knees to my nose

knows ev-'ry-thing a-bout me. The ans-wer is yes, and he

A   Am   D   G   Am

loves me the best, and he knows that my name is *(shout name)*.

B⁷   Em   A⁷   D

Words: Greg Leavers
Music: Greg Leavers, arr. Norman Warren

54 Gather around for the table is spread

Ga - ther a - round for the ta - ble is spread, wel - come the food and

G   Em   Am   D   G   C

rest! Wide is our cir - cle, with Christ at the head,

G   Em   Am   D

he is the ho - noured guest. Learn of his love,

G   C   G   Em

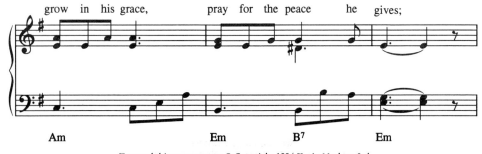

grow in his grace, pray for the peace he gives;

Am   Em   B7   Em

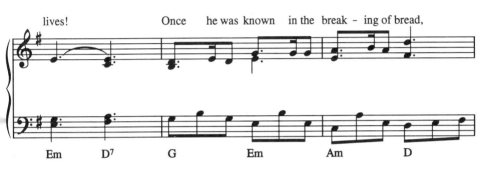

Words: Jean Holloway
Music: traditional Scottish melody, arr. Noel Rawsthorne

55 Give me joy in my heart
Sing hosanna

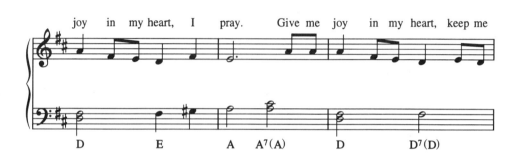

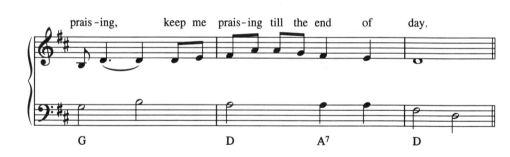

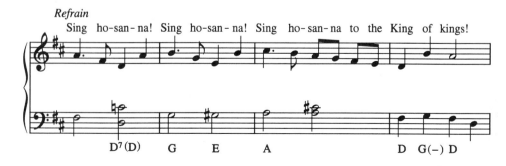

2. Give me peace in my heart, keep me resting,
   give me peace in my heart, I pray.
   Give me peace in my heart, keep me resting,
   keep me resting till the end of day.

3. Give me love in my heart, keep me serving,
   give me love in my heart, I pray.
   Give me love in my heart, keep me serving,
   keep me serving till the end of day.

4. Give me oil in my lamp, keep me burning,
   give me oil in my lamp, I pray.
   Give me oil in my lamp, keep me burning,
   keep me burning till the end of day.

Words: traditional
Music: traditional, arr. John Ballantine

56 Give thanks to the Lord

Refrain

Give thanks to the Lord for he is good. Give thanks to the Lord for

Capo 5   C   Am   C   Am

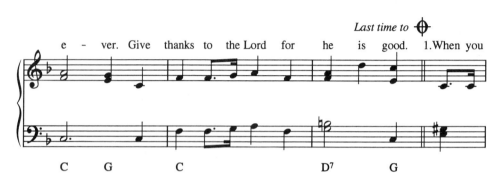

e - ver. Give thanks to the Lord for he is good.   *Last time to*

1. When you

C   G   C   D⁷   G

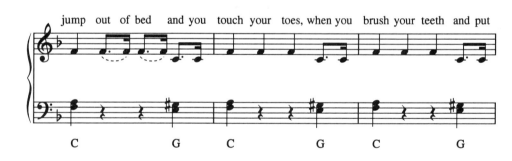

jump out of bed and you touch your toes, when you brush your teeth and put

C   G   C   G   C   G

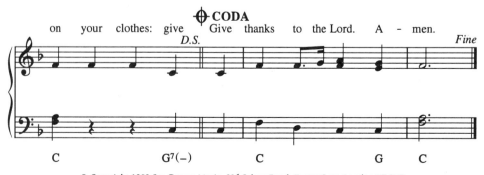

on your clothes: give   **CODA**   Give thanks to the Lord. A - men.

D.S.   *Fine*

C   G⁷(−)   C   G   C

2. When you eat your dinner
   and you're all full up,
   when your mum says *(name)*,
   and you help wash up:

3. When you stretch up high
   and you touch the ground,
   when you stretch out wide
   and you turn around:

4. When you click your fingers
   and you stamp your feet,
   when you clap your hands
   and you slap your knees:

Last refrain:
   Give thanks to the Lord for he is good.
   Give thanks to the Lord for ever.
   Give thanks to the Lord for he is good.
   Give thanks to the Lord. Amen.

Words: Janet Morgan
Music: Janet Morgan, arr. Noel Rawsthorne

57 Give thanks with a grateful heart

Flowing

Give thanks with a grate-ful heart, give thanks to the

G   D   Em

Ho-ly One; give thanks be-cause he's giv-en Je-sus Christ, his

Bm (D)   C   G   F (Dm)

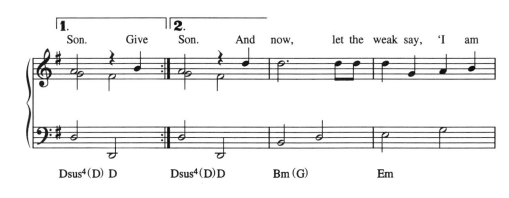

1. Son. Give
2. Son. And now, let the weak say, 'I am

Dsus⁴(D) D   Dsus⁴(D)D   Bm (G)   Em

strong,' let the poor say, 'I am rich,' be-cause of what the Lord has

Am   D⁷   G   Em

done   for   us.   And   now,   let the weak say, 'I   am

F(Dm)   Dsus⁴(D) D   Bm (G)   Em

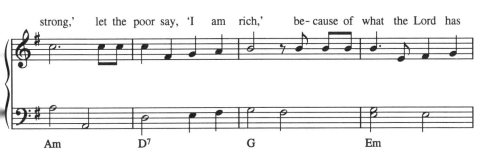

strong,'   let the poor say, 'I   am   rich,'   be-cause of what the Lord has

Am   D⁷   G   Em

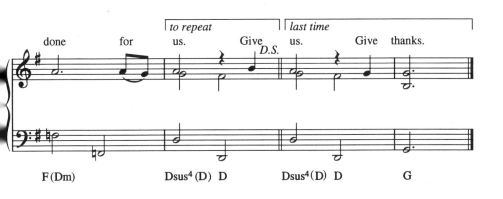

to repeat   *last time*

done   for   us.   Give   us.   Give   thanks.

                D.S.

F(Dm)   Dsus⁴(D) D   Dsus⁴(D) D   G

Words: Henry Smith
Music: Henry Smith, arr. Christopher Tambling

58 Gloria
Clap, clap, clap Gloria

* Clap on each quaver

us;   we wor - ship you,   we   give you thanks,   we

Bm (D)   Em   Em

sing our song of praise.   *D.C.*

Asus⁴(A)   A

2. Jesus, Saviour of all,
   Lord God, Lamb of God,
   you take away our sins, O Lord,
   have mercy on us all.

3. At the Father's right hand,
   Lord, receive our prayer,
   for you alone are the Holy One,
   and you alone are Lord.

4. Glory, Father and Son,
   glory, Holy Spirit,
   to you we raise our hands up high,
   we glorify your name.

Words: Mike Anderson
Music: Mike Anderson, arr. Norman Warren

59 Glory and honour to God in the highest

2. Lord Jesus Christ, only Son of the Father,
   O Lamb of God who takes our transgression away,
   grant us your healing,
   mercy revealing,
   seated in glory, O hear us we pray.

3. You, only you, are the Lord high and holy,
   with God the Holy Spirit exalted above.
   O perfect union,
   blessèd Communion!
   Reign with the Father in glory and love.

Words: Michael Forster
Music: traditional English melody, arr. Noel Rawsthorne

60 Glory, glory in the highest

Brightly

Words: Danny Daniels
Music: Danny Daniels, arr. Christopher Tambling

The
Children's
Hymn
Book

61 Glory to God
Peruvian Gloria

Leader
1. Glo-ry to God, glo-ry to God, glo-ry to the Fa - ther.

All
Glo-ry to God, glo-ry to God, glo-ry to the Fa - ther.

Refrain
Leader / All / Leader
To him be glo-ry for e-ver. **To him be glo-ry for e-ver.** Al-le-lu-ia, a-men.

All
Al-le-lu-ia, a-men, al-le-lu-ia, a-men, al-le-lu-ia, a-men.

2. Glory to God, glory to God,
   Son of the Father.
   Glory to God, glory to God,
   Son of the Father.

3. Glory to God, glory to God,
   Glory to the Spirit.
   Glory to God, glory to God,
   Glory to the Spirit.

This is best sung accompanied only by bongos or a similar percussion instrument.
The optional harmony notes give added effect, but those singing the tune should remain
on the lower notes.

Words: traditional Peruvian
Music: traditional Peruvian, collected and arr. John Ballantine

62 Glory to God, to God in the height
Country Gardens Gloria

1. Glo - ry to God, to God in the height, bring-ing peace to ev - 'ry

C   F (Dm)   G   C   Dm

na - tion. Lord God al-migh - ty, Fa - ther and King, and the

G⁷   C   F (Dm)   G   C

au - thor of sal - va - tion. 'Glo - ry!' let the peo - ple sing,

Dm   G⁷   C   Am   Em

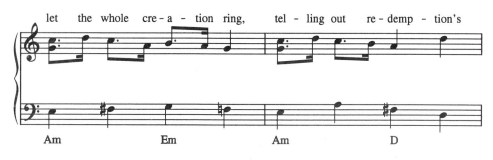

let the whole cre - a - tion ring, tel - ling out re - demp - tion's

Am   Em   Am   D

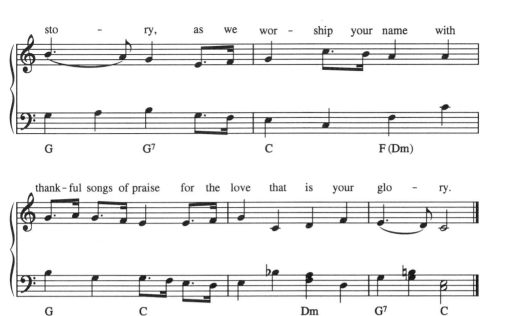

sto - ry, as we wor - ship your name with

G   G⁷   C   F (Dm)

thank-ful songs of praise for the love that is your glo - ry.

G   C   Dm   G⁷   C

2. Jesus, the Father's one holy Son,
   all creation bows before you.
   You are the God, the God we acclaim,
   and we worship and adore you.
   Lamb of God, to you we pray,
   you who take our sin away,
   mercy, grace and truth revealing.
   At the right hand of God, receive our humble prayer
   for forgiveness, hope and healing.

3. You, Jesus Christ, alone are the Lord,
   by your own eternal merit;
   sharing by right the glory of God
   in the presence of the Spirit.
   You alone are Lord Most High,
   you alone we glorify,
   reigning over all creation.
   To the Father, the Son and Spirit, three in one,
   be eternal acclamation!

Words: Michael Forster
Music: traditional English melody, arr. Noel Rawsthorne

63 Go wandering in the sun

2. Just watch a feather fall,
   lay it on your cheek.
   Jesus is as gentle
   with the frightened and the weak.

3. Enjoy the drops of rain,
   sparkling as they fall.
   Jesus is as gen'rous
   with his blessings to us all.

4. Well, can you hold the sea,
   make a living flow'r?
   Neither can we understand
   the greatness of his pow'r.

5. Yet run against the wind –
   very soon you'll see –
   just as strong and free
   is Jesus' love for you and me.

Words: Susan Sayers
Music: Susan Sayers, arr. Noel Rawsthorne

64 God almighty set a rainbow

Refrain after each verse:
Thank you, Father, thank you, Father,
thank you, Father, for your care,
for your warm and loving kindness
to your people ev'rywhere.

2. Clouds will gather, storms come streaming
   on the darkened earth below –
   too much sunshine makes a desert,
   without rain no seed can grow.

3. Through the stormcloud shines your rainbow,
   through the dark earth springs the wheat.
   In the future waits your harvest
   and the food for all to eat.

4. God almighty, you have promised
   after rain the sun will show;
   bless the seeds and bless the harvest.
   Give us grace to help us grow.

Words: Caroline Somerville
Music: traditional melody, arr. Noel Rawsthorne

65 God forgave my sin
Freely, freely

Flowing

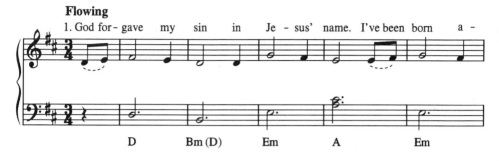

1. God for-gave my sin in Je-sus' name. I've been born a-

D   Bm (D)   Em   A   Em

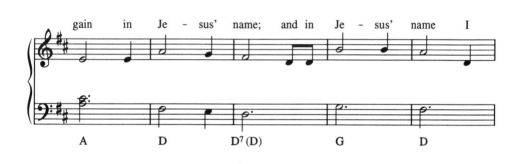

gain in Je-sus' name; and in Je-sus' name I

A   D   D⁷ (D)   G   D

come to you to share his love as he told me

Em   A⁷   D   Bm (D)   F♯m (A)   Em   A⁷

Refrain

to. He said, 'Free - ly, free - ly you have re - ceived;

D   G   A   D   Bm (D)   Em   A⁷

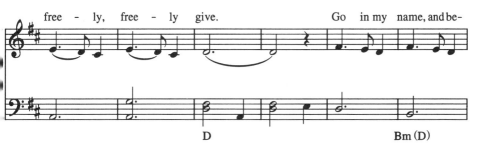

free - ly, free - ly give. Go in my name, and be-

D   Bm (D)

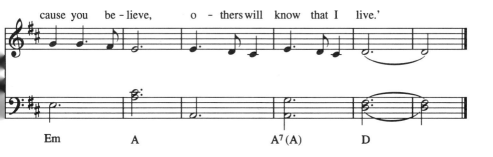

cause you be - lieve, o - thers will know that I live.'

Em   A   A⁷ (A)   D

2. All pow'r is giv'n in Jesus' name,
   in earth and heav'n in Jesus' name;
   and in Jesus' name I come to you
   to share his pow'r as he told me to.

3. God gives us life in Jesus' name,
   he lives in us in Jesus' name;
   and in Jesus' name I come to you
   to share his peace as he told me to.

Words: Carol Owens
Music: Carol Owens, arr. Christopher Tambling

66 God has spoken

Bright and rhythmic

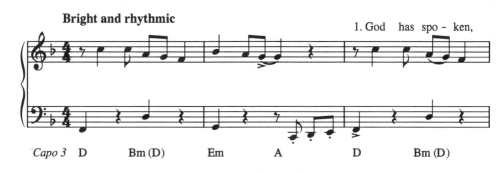

1. God has spo - ken,

Capo 3   D   Bm (D)   Em   A   D   Bm (D)

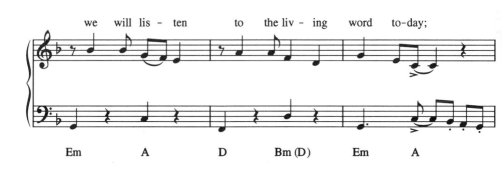

we will lis - ten to the liv - ing word to-day;

Em   A   D   Bm (D)   Em   A

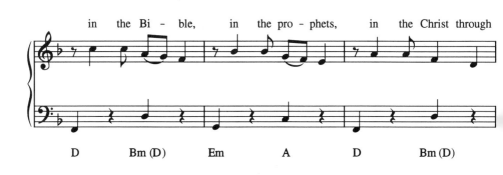

in the Bi - ble, in the pro - phets, in the Christ through

D   Bm (D)   Em   A   D   Bm (D)

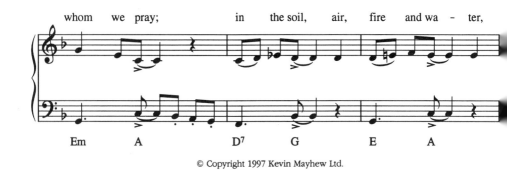

whom we pray; in the soil, air, fire and wa - ter,

Em   A   D⁷   G   E   A

through earth's crea - tures   and   earth's child - ren,   God   still   speaks   to

F♯m (A)   Bm (D)   Em   A   D   G

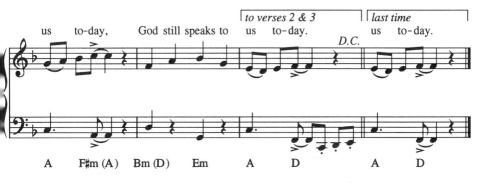

us   to-day,   God still speaks to   us   to-day.   us   to-day.

to verses 2 & 3   *last time*

D.C.

A   F♯m (A)   Bm (D)   Em   A   D   A   D

2. God has spoken, we will listen
   to the living word today;
   in the lovers, in the dreamers,
   in what fearless critics say;
   through the writers, actors, dancers,
   poets, artists, clowns and weavers,
   God still speaks to us today,
   God still speaks to us today.

3. God has spoken, we will listen
   to the living word today;
   through the media, in the text books,
   through our study, work and play;
   on computers, 'phones and faxes,
   through our senses, humour, wisdom,
   God still speaks to us today,
   God still speaks to us today.

Words: W.L. Wallace
Music: Martin Setchell

67 God is the centre and the circle

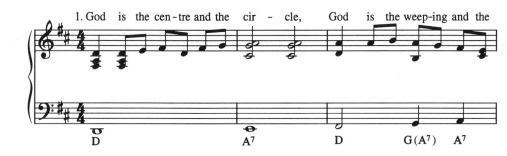

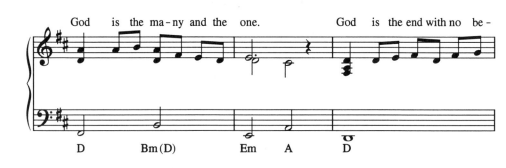

God is the death and God the liv - ing, God is the ma-ny and the one.

G   Em   D   A⁷   D

2. God is the binding and the freedom,
   God is aloneness and embrace,
   God is the peace and God the struggle,
   God is the nameless and the face.
   God is the centre and the circle,
   God is the weeping and the fun,
   God is the dancing and the stillness,
   God is the many and the one.

Words: W.L. Wallace
Music: Andrew Gant

68 God our Father gave us life

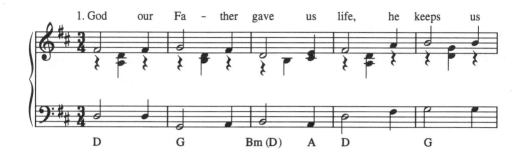

1. God our Fa - ther gave us life, he keeps us

D   G   Bm (D)   A   D   G

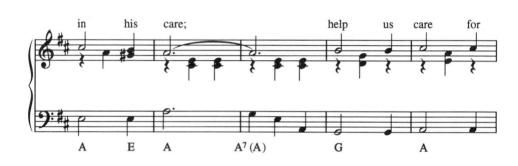

in his care;   help us care for

A   E   A   A⁷ (A)   G   A

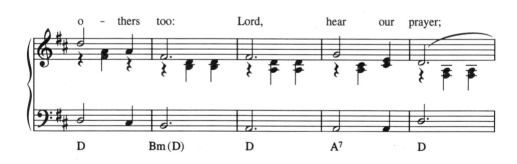

o - thers too: Lord,   hear our prayer;

D   Bm (D)   D   A⁷   D

Lord,   hear our prayer.

A   D   A⁷   D

2. When we're frightened, hurt or tired,
   there's always someone there.
   Make us thankful for their love:
   Lord, hear our prayer;
   Lord, hear our prayer.

3. All God's children need his love,
   a love that we can share.
   So, we pray for ev'ryone:
   Lord, hear our prayer;
   Lord, hear our prayer.

Words: Kathleen Middleton
Music: Kathleen Middleton, arr. Noel Rawsthorne

69 God sends a rainbow
Colours of hope

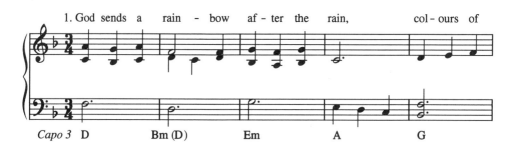

1. God sends a rain-bow af-ter the rain, col-ours of

Capo 3 D   Bm (D)   Em   A   G

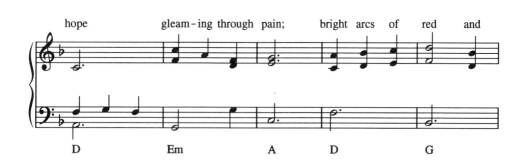

hope gleam-ing through pain; bright arcs of red and

D   Em   A   D   G

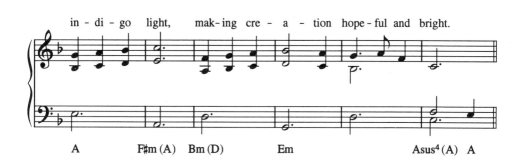

in-di-go light, mak-ing cre-a-tion hope-ful and bright.

A   F#m (A) Bm (D)   Em   Asus⁴(A) A

Refrain
Col-ours of hope dance in the sun, while it yet

D   G   A⁷   D   Bm (D)

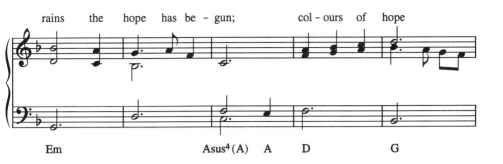

rains the hope has be - gun; col - ours of hope

Em   Asus⁴(A)   A   D   G

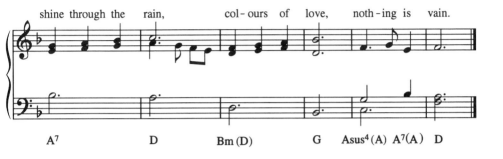

shine through the rain, col - ours of love, noth - ing is vain.

A⁷   D   Bm (D)   G   Asus⁴(A) A⁷(A) D

2. When we are lonely, when we're afraid,
   though it seems dark, rainbows are made;
   even when life itself has to end,
   God is our rainbow, God is our friend.

3. Where people suffer pain or despair,
   God can be seen in those who care;
   even where war and hatred abound,
   rainbows of hope are still to be found.

4. People themselves like rainbows are made,
   colours of hope in us displayed;
   old ones and young ones, women and men,
   all can be part of love's great 'Amen'!

Words: Michael Forster
Music: Christopher Tambling

70 God turned darkness into light

1. God turned dark-ness in-to light, se-pa-ra-ted day from night,

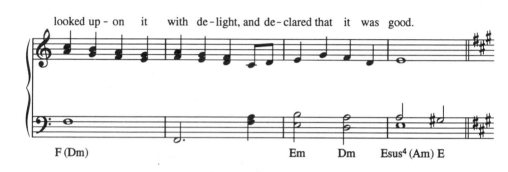

looked up-on it with de-light, and de-clared that it was good.

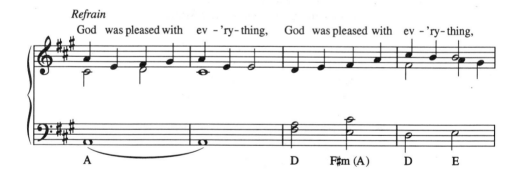

Refrain

God was pleased with ev-'ry-thing, God was pleased with ev-'ry-thing,

God was pleased with ev-'ry-thing, and de-clared that it was good.

2. God divided land and sea,
   filled the world with plants and trees,
   all so beautiful to see,
   and declared that it was good.

3. God made animals galore,
   fishes, birds and dinosaurs,
   heard the splashes, songs and roars,
   and declared that it was good.

4. God made people last of all,
   black and white, and short and tall,
   male and female, large and small,
   and declared that it was good.

Words: Michael Forster
Music: Christopher Tambling

71 God's love is deeper
Deeper, wider, higher

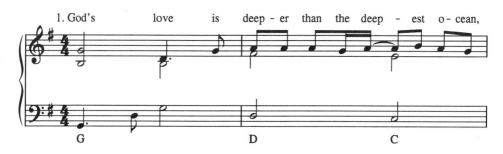

1. God's love is deep-er than the deep-est o-cean,

G D C

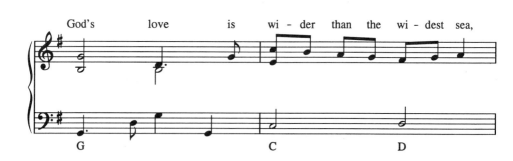

God's love is wi-der than the wi-dest sea,

G C D

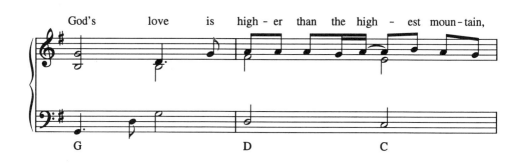

God's love is high-er than the high-est moun-tain,

G D C

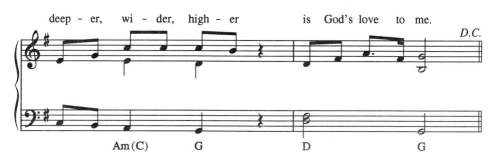

deep-er, wi-der, high-er is God's love to me.

D.C.

Am (C) G D G

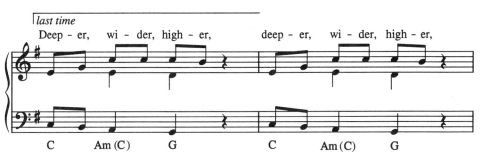

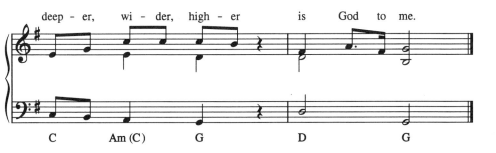

2. God's grace is deeper than the deepest ocean,
   God's grace is wider than the widest sea,
   God's grace is higher than the highest mountain,
   deeper, wider, higher is God's grace to me.

3. God's joy is deeper than the deepest ocean,
   God's joy is wider than the widest sea,
   God's joy is higher than the highest mountain,
   deeper, wider, higher is God's joy to me.

4. God's peace is deeper than the deepest ocean,
   God's peace is wider than the widest sea,
   God's peace is higher than the highest mountain,
   deeper, wider, higher is God's peace to me.
   Deeper, wider, higher,
   deeper, wider, higher,
   deeper, wider, higher is God to me.

Words: Ian D. Craig
Music: Ian D. Craig, arr. Noel Rawsthorne

The
Children's
Hymn
Book

72 God's not dead

Lively

God's not dead. *No! He is a-live. God's not dead. No!

G   C(–)   G   D   C(–)   D

He is a-live. God's not dead. No! He is a-live.

G   C(–)   G

Praise him with my mouth, praise him with my feet, praise him with my hands,

love him in my life. Je-sus is a-live in me.

D⁷   G   C(–)   G

Shout

Words: unknown
Music: unknown, arr. Noel Rawsthorne

This arrangement © Copyright 1997 Kevin Mayhew Ltd.

73 Goliath was big and Goliath was strong
Biggest isn't always best

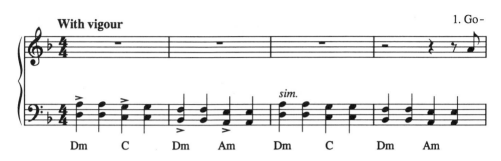

With vigour

Dm　C　Dm　Am　Dm　C　Dm　Am

1. Go-

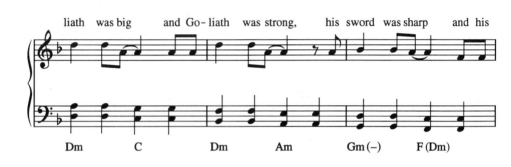

liath was big　and Go-liath　was strong,　his sword was sharp　and his

Dm　C　Dm　Am　Gm (–)　F (Dm)

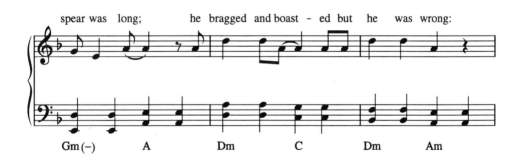

spear was long;　he bragged and boast - ed but he　was wrong:

Gm (–)　A　Dm　C　Dm　Am

big-gest is-n't al - ways　best!　*Refrain*　Big-gest is-n't al - ways

Gm (–)　A　D　B⁷

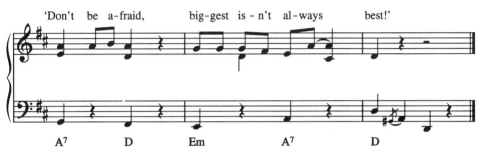

2. A shepherd boy had a stone and sling;
   he killed Goliath and amazed the king!
   The people cheered and began to sing:
   'Biggest isn't always best!'

3. So creatures made in a smaller size,
   like tiny sparrows and butterflies,
   are greater than we may realise:
   biggest isn't always best!

Words: Michael Forster
Music: Christopher Tambling

74 Great indeed are your works

Refrain
Great in-deed are your works, O Lord,   now and e - ver-

Capo 5   C   D⁷   G⁷

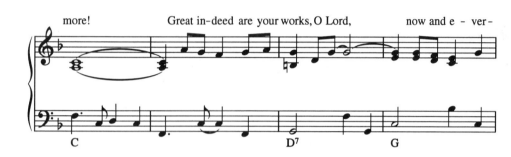

more!   Great in-deed are your works, O Lord,   now and e - ver-

C   D⁷   G

to verses 1 - 3   *last time*
more!   more!   *Fine*   1.The un-i-verse, night and day,

C   C   Dm

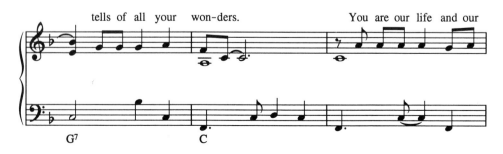

tells of all your won-ders.   You are our life and our

G⁷   C

2. You are the path which we tread,
   you will lead us onward.
   From ev'ry corner of earth
   all the nations gather.

3. You lead them all by the hand
   to the heav'nly kingdom.
   Then, at the end of all time,
   you will come in glory.

Words: Aniceto Nazareth
Music: Aniceto Nazareth, arr. Noel Rawsthorne

75 Halle, halle, halle

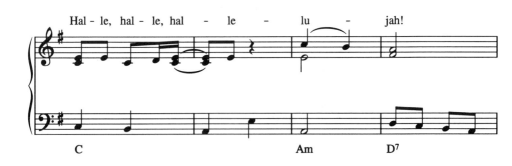

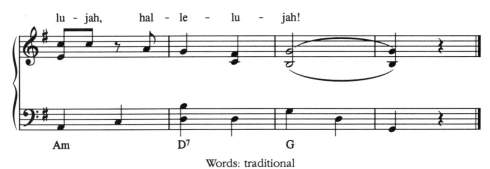

Words: traditional
Music: unknown, arr. Noel Rawsthorne

This arrangement © Copyright 1997 Kevin Mayhew Ltd.

76 Hallelu, hallelu

Words: unknown
Music: unknown, arr. Noel Rawsthorne

77 Hang on

push, don't shove, don't move, that's right, just wait for the Spi - rit of God.

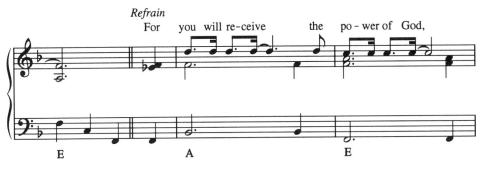

Refrain
For you will re-ceive the po - wer of God,

E   A   E

you will re-ceive the po -wer of God, you will re -ceive the

B⁷   E   A

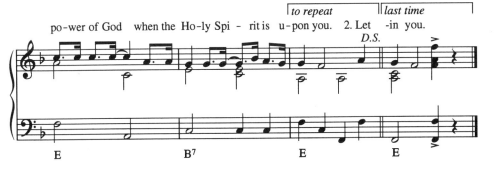

po-wer of God when the Ho-ly Spi - rit is u-pon you. 2. Let -in you.

to repeat   *last time*
D.S.

E   B⁷   E   E

2. Let go, launch out,
   press on, don't fight;
   be filled with the Spirit of God.
   Move on, make way,
   step out, that's right;
   be filled with the Spirit of God.
   (Repeat)

Last refrain:
For you have received the power of God,
you have received the power of God,
you have received the power of God,
now the Holy Spirit lives within you.

Words: Richard Hubbard
Music: Richard Hubbard, arr. Norman Warren

78 Have you heard the raindrops
Water of life

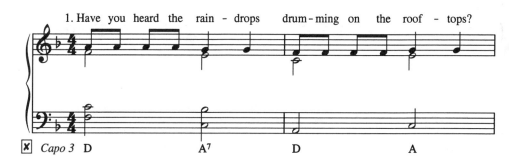

1. Have you heard the rain-drops drum-ming on the roof-tops?

Capo 3 D A⁷ D A

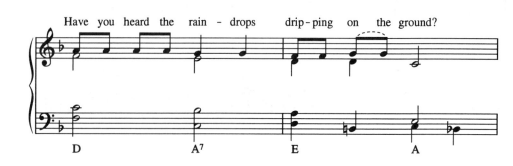

Have you heard the rain-drops drip-ping on the ground?

D A⁷ E A

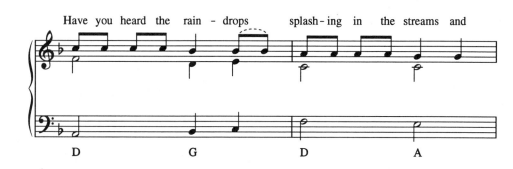

Have you heard the rain-drops splash-ing in the streams and

D G D A

run-ning to the ri-vers all a-round? *Refrain* There's wa - ter,

D A D Bm

2. There's a busy worker digging in the desert,
   digging with a spade that flashes in the sun;
   soon there will be water rising in the well-shaft,
   spilling from the bucket as it comes.

3. Nobody can live who hasn't any water,
   when the land is dry, then nothing much grows;
   Jesus gives us life if we drink the living water,
   sing it so that ev'rybody knows.

Words: Christian Strover
Music: Christian Strover, arr. Noel Rawsthorne

79 He gave me eyes so I could see
He made me

1. He gave me eyes so I could see the won-ders of the world. With-out my eyes I could not see the oth-er boys and girls. He gave me ears so I could hear the wind and rain and sea. I've got to tell it to the world: he made me.

2. He gave me lips so I could speak
and say what's in my mind.
Without my lips I could not speak
a single word or line.
He made my mind so I could think,
and choose what I should be.
I've got to tell it to the world:
he made me.

3. He gave me hands so I could touch,
   and hold a thousand things.
   I need my hands to help me write,
   to help me fetch and bring.
   These feet he made so I could run,
   he meant me to be free.
   I've got to tell it to the world:
   he made me.

Words: Alan Pinnock
Music: Alan Pinnock, arr. Noel Rawsthorne

80 He is the King

Words: unknown
Music: unknown, arr. Noel Rawsthorne

81 He was born in the winter

Calypso style

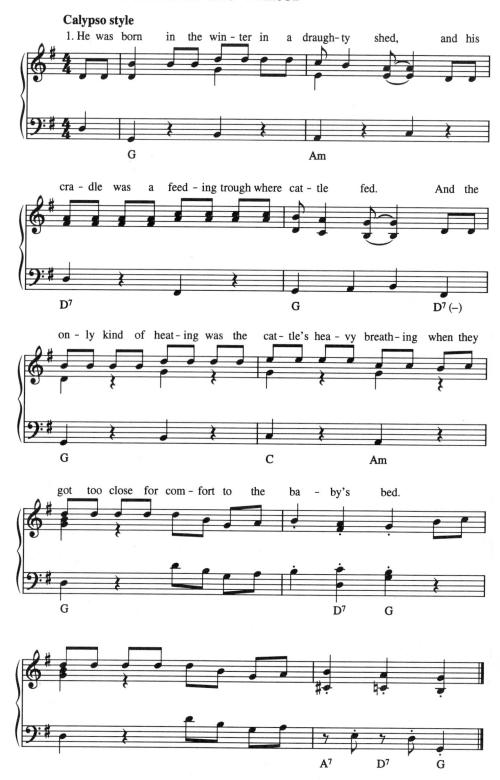

2. He was trained as a carpenter,
   his father's trade,
   but there's no one who remembers
   anything he made,
   for he left his friends and neighbours
   and his profitable labours,
   and he went to be a preacher
   who was never paid!

3. He was friends with the guilty,
   and he helped the poor,
   and he told them all that heaven
   had an open door,
   but the government said, 'Never!
   Better silence him for ever,
   just in case he starts a riot
   or a civil war.'

4. He was whipped by the soldiers
   at the city hall,
   and they nailed him to a wooden cross
   outside the wall.
   They ignored the people crying
   as they stood and watched him dying,
   then they took him down and buried him
   and said, 'That's all!'

5. He was back three days later,
   and his word is clear:
   that he means to live for ever
   and be always here.
   And the promise that he's giving
   is the joy of simply living
   in a world of truth and freedom
   where there's no more fear.

Words: Michael Forster
Music: Christopher Tambling

82 He's got the whole world in his hand

2. He's got you and me, brother, in his hand. (3)
   He's got the whole world in his hand.

3. He's got you and me, sister, in his hand. (3)
   He's got the whole world in his hand.

4. He's got the tiny little baby in his hand. (3)
   He's got the whole world in his hand.

5. He's got ev'rybody here in his hand. (3)
   He's got the whole world in his hand.

Words: traditional
Music: traditional, arr. Alan Ridout

83 He's the same today

Words: S.E. Cox
Music: S.E. Cox, arr. Norman Warren

84 Hear what God says
I have loved you

Gently

Hear what God says to you and ev-'ry-one, hear what God says to you in his word: 'I have loved you with an e-ver-last-ing love, I have loved you with an e-ver-last-ing love.'

Capo 5

C   G   D   G

Am   D⁷   G   D⁷   G⁷   C

G   D   G   D⁷   G   C   G

Words: Eileen Russell
Music: Eileen Russell, arr. Norman Warren

85 Hey, now, everybody sing

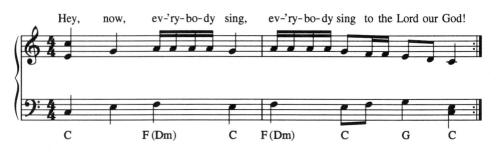

Hey, now, ev-'ry-bo-dy sing, ev-'ry-bo-dy sing to the Lord our God!

C   F (Dm)   C   F (Dm)   C   G   C

Words: Orien Johnson
Music: Orien Johnson, arr. Noel Rawsthorne

86 Ho, ho, ho, hosanna

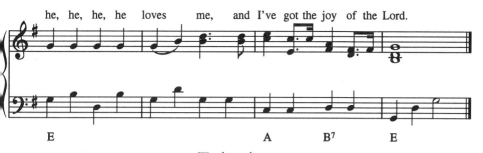

he, he, he, he loves me, and I've got the joy of the Lord.

E   A   B⁷   E

Words: unknown
Music: unknown, arr. Noel Rawsthorne

87 Holy God

Prayerfully

Ho-ly God, we place our-selves in-to your hands. Bless us and care for

C   G   Am   Gsus⁴ G   C   Dm
                             (G)

us, be gra-cious and lov-ing to us; look

A   A⁷(A)   Dm   F(Dm) G   C   Am

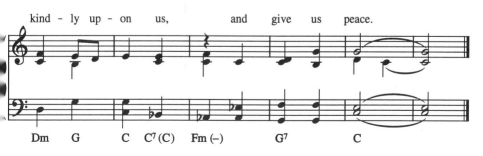

kind - ly up - on us, and give us peace.

Dm   G   C   C⁷(C)   Fm (–)   G⁷   C

Words: adapted by Kevin Mayhew from the Aaronic Blessing
Music: Kevin Mayhew, arr. Noel Rawsthorne

88 Holy, holy, holy is the Lord

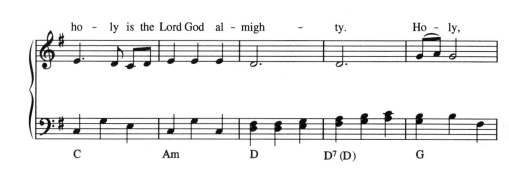

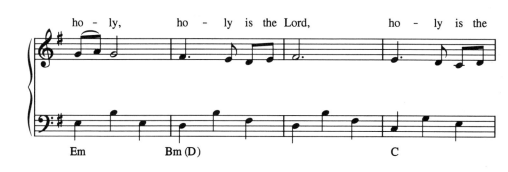

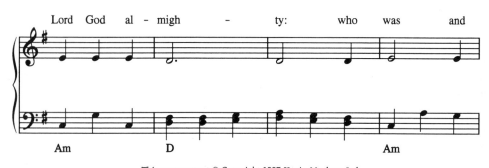

2. Jesus, Jesus, Jesus is the Lord,
   Jesus is the Lord God almighty.
   Jesus, Jesus, Jesus is the Lord,
   Jesus is the Lord God almighty:
   who was and is and is to come;
   Jesus, Jesus, Jesus is the Lord.

3. Worthy, worthy, worthy is the Lord,
   worthy is the Lord God almighty.
   Worthy, worthy, worthy is the Lord,
   worthy is the Lord God almighty:
   who was and is and is to come;
   worthy, worthy, worthy is the Lord.

4. Glory, glory, glory to the Lord,
   glory to the Lord God almighty.
   Glory, glory, glory to the Lord,
   glory to the Lord God almighty:
   who was and is and is to come;
   glory, glory, glory to the Lord.

Words: unknown
Music: unknown, arr. Noel Rawsthorne

89 Holy, most holy, all holy the Lord
Skye Sanctus

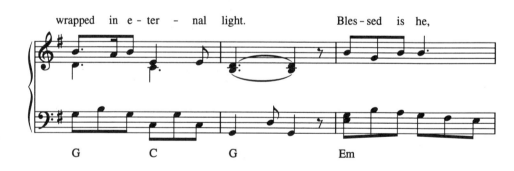

Words: Michael Forster
Music: traditional Scottish melody, arr. Noel Rawsthorne

90 Holy, most holy, all holy the Lord
Slane Sanctus

2. Blessèd, most blessèd, all blessèd is he
whose life makes us whole and whose death sets us free;
who comes in the name of the Father of light,
let endless hosannas resound in the height!

Words: Michael Forster
Music: traditional Irish melody, arr. Alan Ridout

91 Hosanna, hosanna, hosanna in the highest

Lively

1. Ho-san-na, ho-san-na, ho-san-na in the high - est! Ho-san - na, ho-san - na, ho-san-na in the high - est!

Lord, we lift up your name with hearts full of praise; be ex-alt-ed, O Lord my God! Ho-san-na in the high - est!

2. Glory, glory,
glory to the King of kings!
Glory, glory,
glory to the King of kings!
Lord, we lift up your name
with hearts full of praise;
be exalted, O Lord my God!
Glory to the King of kings!

Words: Carl Tuttle, based on Matthew 21:9
Music: Carl Tuttle, arr. Christopher Tambling

92 How did Moses cross the Red Sea?

drive? No! No! Did he fly? No! No! How did he get a -

G   A⁷

cross?   God blew with his wind, puff, puff, puff, puff, he

D   D⁷ (D)   G   C

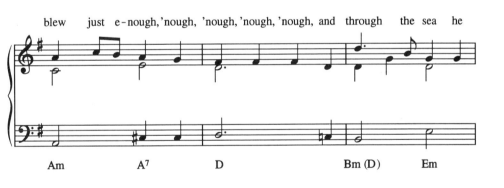

blew just e-nough, 'nough, 'nough, 'nough, 'nough, and through the sea he

Am   A⁷   D   Bm (D)   Em

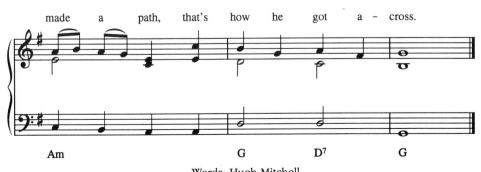

made a path, that's how he got a - cross.

Am   G   D⁷   G

Words: Hugh Mitchell
Music: traditional melodies, adapted by Hugh Mitchell, arr. Noel Rawsthorne

93 How great is our God

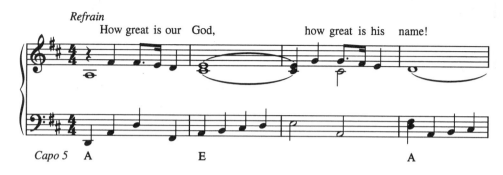

Refrain

How great is our God, how great is his name!

Capo 5 A   E   A

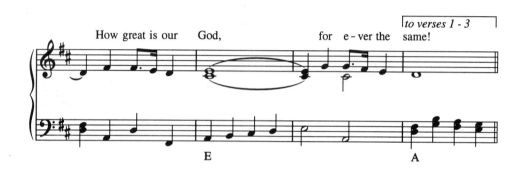

How great is our God, for e-ver the same!

to verses 1 - 3

E   A

last time
same!   *Fine*   1. He rolled back the wa - ters

A

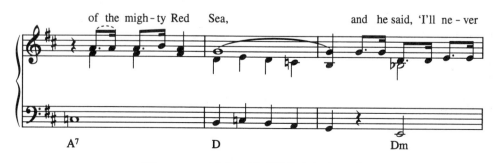

of the migh-ty Red Sea, and he said, 'I'll ne-ver

A^7 D   Dm

2. He sent his Son, Jesus,
   to set us all free,
   and he said, 'I'll never leave you.
   Put your trust in me.'

3. He gave us his Spirit,
   and now we can see.
   And he said, 'I'll never leave you.
   Put your trust in me.'

Words: unknown
Music: unknown, arr. Noel Rawsthorne

94 I am cold, I am ice

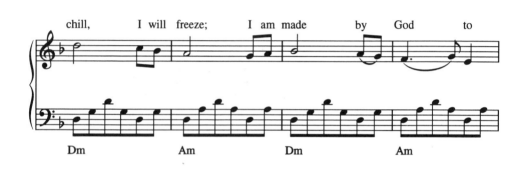

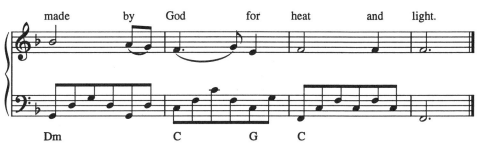

made by God for heat and light.

Dm   C   G   C

2. I am frost, I am snow,
   I will sparkle and shine;
   I am made by God
   to clean the earth.

3. I am rain, I am hail,
   I will drive, I will splash;
   I am made by God
   to feed the earth.

4. I am air, I am wind,
   I will move, I will blow;
   I am made by God
   to clean the sky.

5. I am sun, I am fire,
   I will warm with my flames;
   I am made by God
   for heat and light.

Words: W.L. Wallace
Music: James Patten

95 I come like a beggar

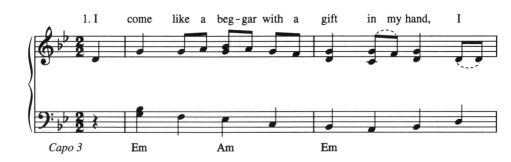

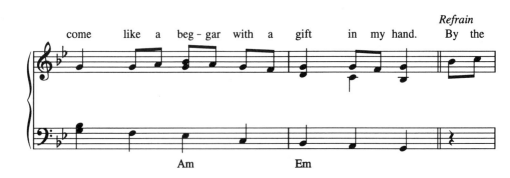

2. I come like a prisoner to set you free,
   I come like a prisoner to set you free.

3. The need of another is the gift that I bring,
   the need of another is the gift that I bring.

4. I come like a beggar, what you do for my sake
   is the wine that I offer you, the bread that I break.

Words: Sydney Carter
Music: Sydney Carter, arr. Noel Rawsthorne

96 I danced in the morning
Lord of the Dance

lead   you   all,   wher - e - ver   you   may   be,   and   I'll

G   Em   Bm (D)   G

lead   you   all   in   the   dance,   said   he.

Am   D⁷   G   C(−)   G

2. I danced for the scribe and the pharisee,
   but they would not dance and they wouldn't follow me.
   I danced for the fishermen, for James and John –
   they came with me and the dance went on.

3. I danced on the Sabbath and I cured the lame;
   the holy people said it was a shame.
   They whipped and they stripped and they hung me on high,
   and they left me there on a cross to die.

4. I danced on a Friday when the sky turned black –
   it's hard to dance with the devil on your back.
   They buried my body, and they thought I'd gone,
   but I am the dance, and I still go on.

5. They cut me down and I leapt up high;
   I am the life that'll never, never die;
   I'll live in you if you'll live in me –
   I am the Lord of the Dance, said he.

Words: Sydney Carter
Music: traditional American melody adapted by Sydney Carter, arr. Noel Rawsthorne

97 I feel spring in the air today
Spring in the air

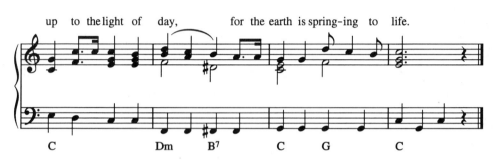

Brightly

1. I feel spring in the air to-day, lots of flow-ers are on their way, burst-ing

up to the light of day, for the earth is spring-ing to life.

2. I feel spring in the air today,
   lambs are ready to frisk and play;
   nests are built as the tall trees sway,
   for the earth is springing to life.

3. I feel spring in the air today,
   Lord and Father, I want to say
   thanks for showing your love this way,
   for the earth is springing to life.

Words: Susan Sayers
Music: Noel Rawsthorne

98 I gotta home in gloryland

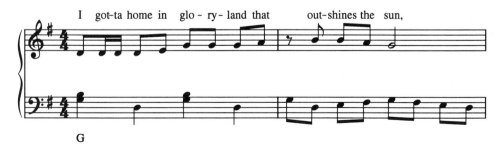

I got-ta home in glo - ry- land that out-shines the sun,

Words: traditional
Music: traditional, arr. Noel Rawsthorne

The
Children's
Hymn
Book

99 I have a friend

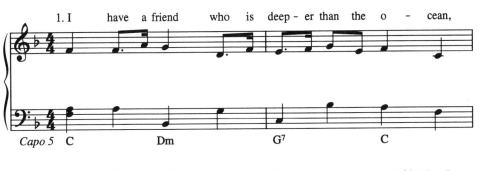

2. If I am lost he will search until he finds me,
   if I am scared he will help me to be brave.
   All I've to do is to turn to him and ask him.
   I know he'll honour the promise he gave.

3. 'Don't be afraid,' Jesus said, 'for I am with you.'
   'Don't be afraid,' Jesus said, 'for I am here.
   Now and for ever, anywhere you travel,
   I shall be with you, I'll always be near.'

Words: Susan Sayers
Music: Susan Sayers, arr. Noel Rawsthorne
© Copyright 1986 Kevin Mayhew Ltd.

100 I love to be with you
To be with you

1. I love to be with you, Je - sus, list'n - ing to your

D A⁷ D A⁷

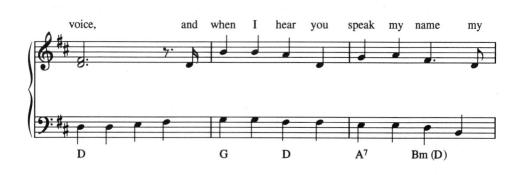

voice, and when I hear you speak my name my

D G D A⁷ Bm (D)

heart and soul re - joice. And if you said jump, I'd jump for you, and

Em A D Bm (D) G A

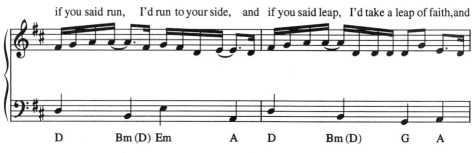

if you said run, I'd run to your side, and if you said leap, I'd take a leap of faith, and

D Bm (D) Em A D Bm (D) G A

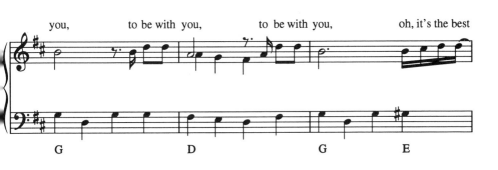

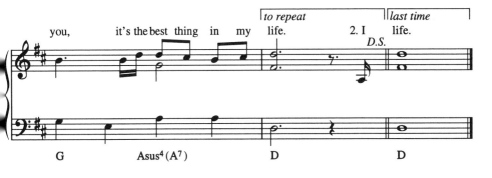

Words: Mike Burn
Music: Mike Burn, arr. Noel Rawsthorne

101 I reach up high

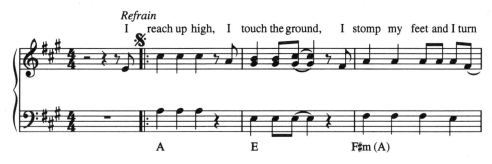

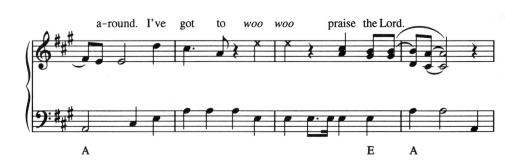

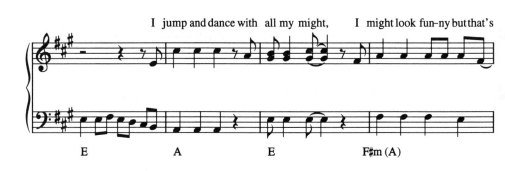

2. May my whole life be a song of praise,
   to worship God in ev'ry way.
   In this song the actions praise his name,
   I want my actions ev'ry day to do the same.

Words: Judy Bailey
Music: Judy Bailey, arr. Norman Warren

102 I, the Lord of sea and sky
Here I am, Lord

2. I, the Lord of snow and rain,
   I have borne my people's pain.
   I have wept for love of them.
   They turn away.
   I will break their hearts of stone,
   give them hearts for love alone.
   I will speak my word to them.
   Whom shall I send?

3. I, the Lord of wind and flame,
   I will tend the poor and lame.
   I will set a feast for them.
   My hand will save.
   Finest bread I will provide,
   till their hearts are satisfied.
   I will give my life to them.
   Whom shall I send?

Words: Dan Schutte, based on Isaiah 6
Music: Dan Schutte, arr. Noel Rawsthorne

103 I was so glad

Leader
1. I was so glad,

All
I was so glad,

Leader
when they said to me,

Capo 5 Em   C   Am   Em

All
when they said to me,

Leader
'Let us go up,

All
let us go up,

D   Em   C

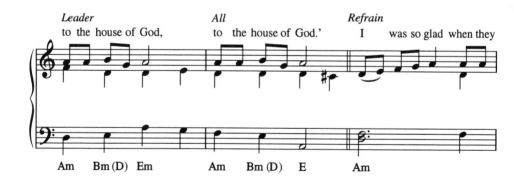

Leader
to the house of God,

All
to the house of God.'

Refrain
I was so glad when they

Am   Bm (D)   Em   Am   Bm (D)   E   Am

said to me, 'Let us go up to the house of God.'

D   Am   Dm   G   Dm

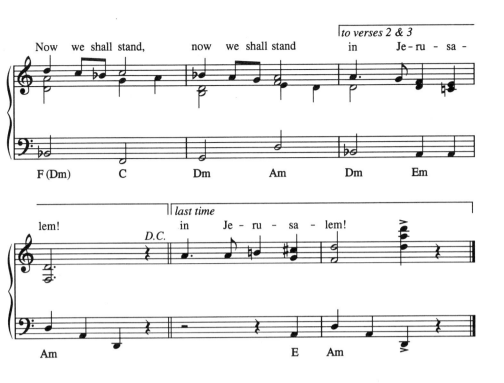

2. Solidly built,
   solidly built,
   is Jerusalem,
   is Jerusalem.
   There we shall go,
   there we shall go,
   people of the Lord,
   people of the Lord.

3. Here by his law,
   here by his law,
   God is glorified,
   God is glorified.
   Judgement is his,
   judgement is his,
   on King David's throne,
   on King David's throne.

Words: Michael Forster, based on Psalm 121
Music: Norman Warren

104 I will be with you

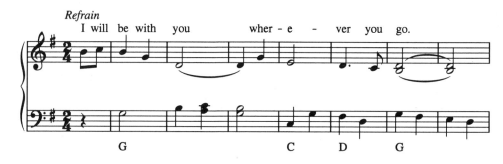

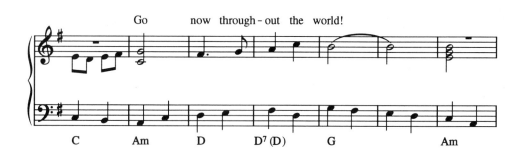

2. And you, my friend, will you now leave me,
   or do you know me as your Lord?

3. Your life will be transformed with power
   by living truly in my name.

4. And if you say, 'Yes, Lord, I love you,'
   then feed my lambs and feed my sheep.

Words: Gerard Markland
Music: Gerard Markland, arr. Noel Rawsthorne

105 I will click my fingers

I will click my fin - gers, clap my hands, stamp my feet and

Getting faster

Capo 1 A D E

shout ha - le - lu - jah! Then I'll whis - tle as loud as I can. *(Whistle)*

A D

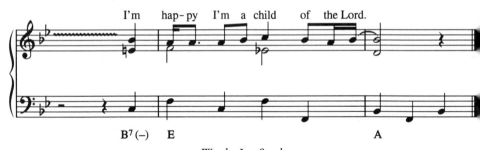

I'm hap - py I'm a child of the Lord.

B⁷ (–) E A

Words: Ian Smale
Music: Ian Smale, arr. Noel Rawsthorne

© Copyright 1989 Glorie Music/Kingsway's Thankyou Music, P.O. Box 75, Eastbourne, East Sussex BN23 6NW, UK.
Worldwide. Used by permission.

106 I will enter his gates
He has made me glad

With pace and swing

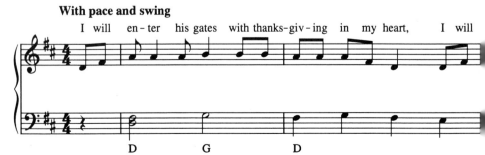

I will en - ter his gates with thanks-giv - ing in my heart, I will

D G D

© Copyright 1976 Maranatha! Music, administered by CopyCare, P.O. Box 77, Hailsham BN27 3EF UK.
Used by permission.

Words: Leona von Brethorst
Music: Leona von Brethorst, arr. Christopher Tambling

107 I will sing, I will sing

Capo 3

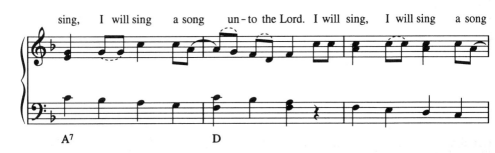

2. We will come, we will come as one before the Lord.
We will come, we will come as one before the Lord.
We will come, we will come as one before the Lord.
Alleluia, glory to the Lord.

3. If the Son, if the Son shall make you free,
if the Son, if the Son shall make you free,
if the Son, if the Son shall make you free,
you shall be free indeed.

4. They that sow in tears shall reap in joy.
   They that sow in tears shall reap in joy.
   They that sow in tears shall reap in joy.
   Alleluia, glory to the Lord.

5. Ev'ry knee shall bow and ev'ry tongue confess,
   Ev'ry knee shall bow and ev'ry tongue confess,
   Ev'ry knee shall bow and ev'ry tongue confess
   that Jesus Christ is Lord.

6. In his name, in his name we have the victory.
   In his name, in his name we have the victory.
   In his name, in his name we have the victory.
   Alleluia, glory to the Lord.

Words: Max Dyer
Music: Max Dyer, arr. Noel Rawsthorne

108 I will wave my hands

Lively

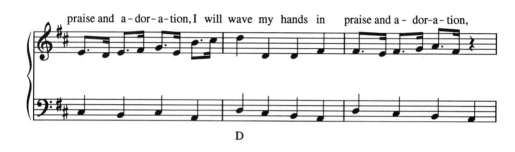

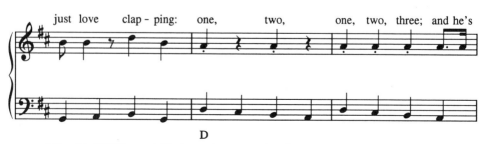

Words: Ian Smale
Music: Ian Smale, arr. Noel Rawsthorne

109 I'm accepted, I'm forgiven

Words: Rob Hayward
Music: Rob Hayward, arr. Christopher Tambling

110 I'm black, I'm white, I'm short, I'm tall

Fast

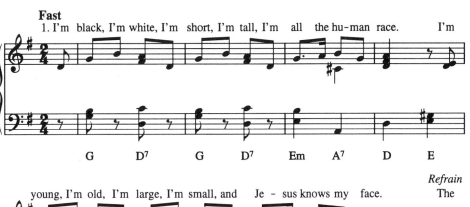

1. I'm black, I'm white, I'm short, I'm tall, I'm all the hu-man race. I'm

G   D7   G   D7   Em   A7   D   E

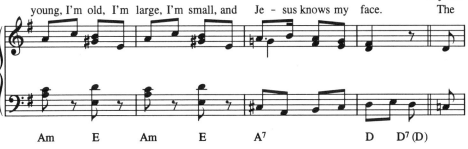

young, I'm old, I'm large, I'm small, and Je - sus knows my face. The

Refrain

Am   E   Am   E   A7   D   D7 (D)

love of God is free to ev - 'ry-one, free to ev - 'ry-one, free to ev - 'ry-one.

G   Em   Am   D7   G   C   Am   B7

The love of God is free, oh yes! That's what the gos-pel says.

Em   G   C   Am   D   D7 (D)   G

2.   I'm rich, I'm poor, I'm pleased, I'm sad,
I'm ev'ryone you see.
I'm quick, I'm slow, I'm good, I'm bad,
I know that God loves me.

3.   So tall and thin, and short and wide,
and any shade of face,
I'm one of those for whom Christ died,
part of the human race.

Words: Michael Forster
Music: Christopher Tambling

111 I'm glad I'm alive

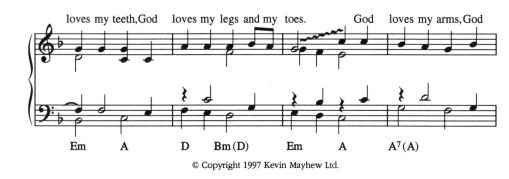

loves my fing - ers, God loves my tum-my and my nose. I'm

F#(C#dim⁷) Bm (D)   G   A   D   G(−) D A⁷(−)

2. I love my lips, yes, I love my teeth,
   I love my legs and my toes.
   I love my arms, I love my fingers,
   I love my tummy and my nose.

Words: W.L. Wallace
Music: Richard Lloyd

112 I'm gonna click

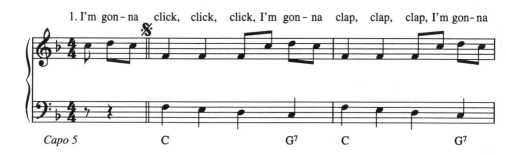

1. I'm gon-na click, click, click, I'm gon-na clap, clap, clap, I'm gon-na

Capo 5   C   G⁷   C   G⁷

click, I'm gon-na clap and praise the Lord!   Be-

C   G

cause of all he's done, I'm gon-na make him 'Num-ber One'. I'm gon-na

C   Am   Dm   D⁷

to verses 2 - 4   *last time*

click, I'm gon-na clap and praise the Lord!   2. I'm gon-na Lord!

D.S.

C   G⁷   C   C

2. I'm gonna zoom, zoom, zoom
   around the room, room, room,
   I'm gonna zoom around the room and praise the Lord!
   Because of all he's done,
   I'm gonna make him 'Number One'.
   I'm gonna zoom around the room and praise the Lord!

3. I'm gonna sing, sing, sing,
   I'm gonna shout, shout, shout,
   I'm gonna sing, I'm gonna shout and praise the Lord!
   Because of all he's done,
   I'm gonna make him 'Number One'.
   I'm gonna sing, I'm gonna shout and praise the Lord!

4. I'm gonna click, click, click,
   I'm gonna clap, clap, clap,
   I'm gonna click, I'm gonna clap and praise the Lord!
   Because of all he's done,
   I'm gonna make him 'Number One'.
   I'm gonna click, I'm gonna clap and praise the Lord!

Words: Alan J. Price
Music: Alan J. Price, arr. Noel Rawsthorne

The
Children's
Hymn
Book

113 I've got peace like a river

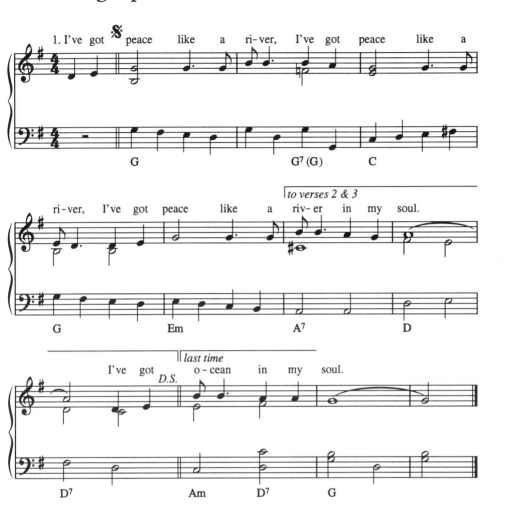

2. I've got joy like a fountain,
   I've got joy like a fountain,
   I've got joy like a fountain in my soul.

3. I've got love like an ocean,
   I've got love like an ocean,
   I've got love like an ocean in my soul.

Words: Spiritual
Music: Spiritual, arr. Noel Rawsthorne

114 If I were a butterfly

Refrain

For you gave me a heart, and you gave me a smile, you gave me Je-sus and you made me your child, and I just thank you, Fa-ther, for mak-ing me 'me'.

G   A   D

2. If I were an elephant,
    I'd thank you, Lord, by raising my trunk,
    and if I were a kangaroo,
    you know I'd hop right up to you,
    and if I were an octopus,
    I'd thank you, Lord, for my fine looks,
    but I just thank you, Father, for making me 'me'.

3. If I were a wiggly worm,
    I'd thank you, Lord, that I could squirm,
    and if I were a billy goat,
    I'd thank you, Lord, for my strong throat,
    and if I were a fuzzy wuzzy bear,
    I'd thank you, Lord, for my fuzzy wuzzy hair,
    but I just thank you, Father, for making me 'me'.

Words: Brian Howard
Music: Brian Howard, arr. Noel Rawsthorne

115 If I were an astronaut

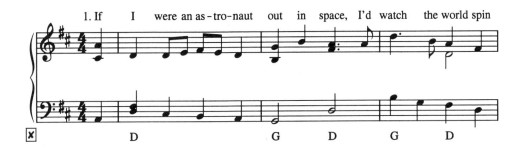

1. If I were an as-tro-naut out in space, I'd watch the world spin by,

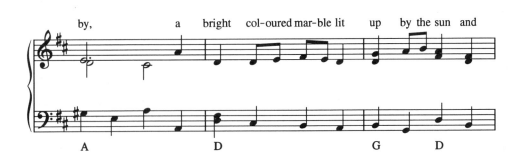

a bright col-oured mar-ble lit up by the sun and

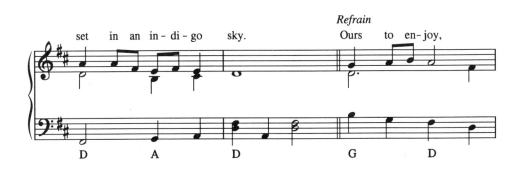

set in an in-di-go sky. *Refrain* Ours to en-joy,

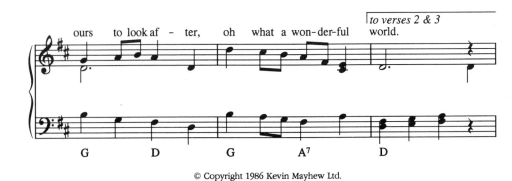

ours to look af-ter, oh what a won-der-ful world. *to verses 2 & 3*

2. If I were a monkey, and treetop high,
   I'd see the fruits that grow,
   delicious and succulent, fragrant and sweet,
   on branches above and below.

3. If I were an octopus in the sea,
   the sun would filter through
   to dapple the corals and brighten the shells
   down deep in an ocean of blue.

Words: Susan Sayers
Music: Susan Sayers, arr. Noel Rawsthorne

116 In the first stage of seeking
Seven stages of spiritual growth

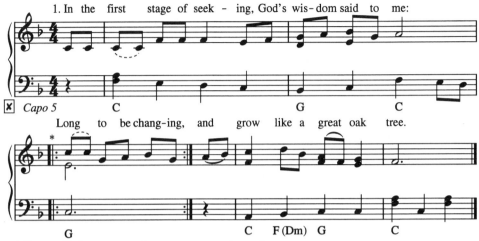

1. In the first stage of seek - ing, God's wis- dom said to me:

Capo 5

Long to be chang-ing, and grow like a great oak tree.

* *Repeat this bar as many times as necessary for each verse*

2. In the second stage of seeking,
   God's wisdom said to me:
   Trust in your spirit,
   long to be changing,
   and grow like a great oak tree.

3. In the third stage of seeking,
   God's wisdom said to me:
   Live with the chaos,
   trust in your spirit,
   long to be changing,
   and grow like a great oak tree.

4. In the fourth stage of seeking,
   God's wisdom said to me:
   Let go of all things,
   live with the chaos,
   trust in your spirit,
   long to be changing,
   and grow like a great oak tree.

5. In the fifth stage of seeking,
   God's wisdom said to me:
   Dance in the wonder,
   let go of all things,
   live with the chaos,
   trust in your spirit,
   long to be changing,
   and grow like a great oak tree.

6. In the sixth stage of seeking,
   God's wisdom said to me:
   Flow'r through each dying,
   dance in the wonder,
   let go of all things,
   live with the chaos,
   trust in your spirit,
   long to be changing,
   and grow like a great oak tree.

7. In the seventh stage of seeking,
   God's wisdom said to me:
   Merge with the myst'ry,
   flow'r through each dying,
   dance in the wonder,
   let go of all things,
   live with the chaos,
   trust in your spirit,
   long to be changing,
   and grow like a great oak tree.

Words: W.L. Wallace
Music: traditional English melody, arr. Noel Rawsthorne

117 In the upper room
You must do for others

2. Peter was annoyed: 'This will never do!
   You, as Master, should not play the servant!'
   Jesus took a towel, knelt to dry their feet,
   told them:
   'You must do for others as I do for you.'

Words: Gerard Fitzpatrick
Music: Gerard Fitzpatrick, arr. Noel Rawsthorne

118 Isn't it good

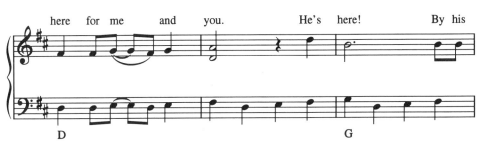

Words: Alan J. Price
Music: Alan J. Price, arr. Noel Rawsthorne

119 It's me, O Lord
Standing in the need of prayer

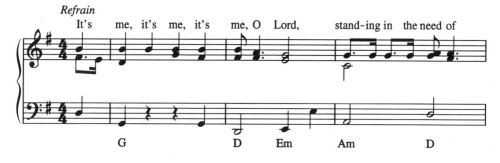

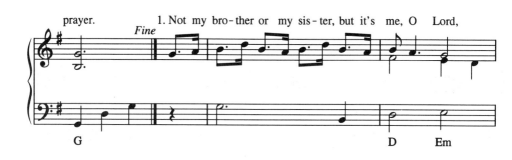

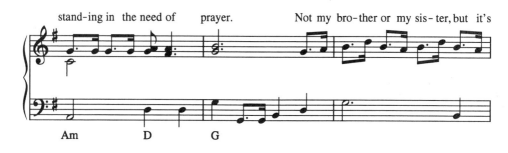

2. Not my mother or my father,
   but it's me, O Lord,
   standing in the need of prayer.
   Not my mother or my father,
   but it's me, O Lord,
   standing in the need of prayer.

3. Not the stranger or my neighbour,
   but it's me, O Lord,
   standing in the need of prayer.
   Not the stranger or my neighbour,
   but it's me, O Lord,
   standing in the need of prayer.

Words: Spiritual
Music: Spiritual, arr. Noel Rawsthorne

120 Jesus calls us to a party
Just a little bit of bread and a little bit of wine

1. Je-sus calls us to a par-ty where he gives us sim-ple

G   Em   Am   D⁷   G   A⁷

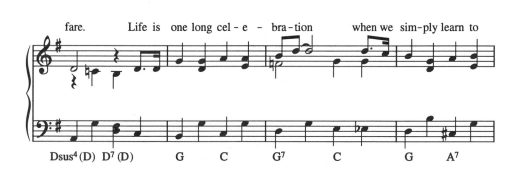

fare.   Life is one long cel-e-bra-tion when we sim-ply learn to

Dsus⁴(D) D⁷(D)   G   C   G⁷   C   G   A⁷

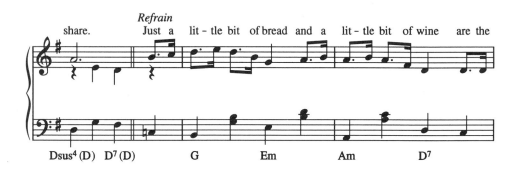

share.   *Refrain*   Just a lit-tle bit of bread and a lit-tle bit of wine are the

Dsus⁴(D) D⁷(D)   G   Em   Am   D⁷

on-ly things we need.   Just a lit-tle bit of bread and a

G   A⁷   Dsus⁴(D) D⁷(D)   G   Em

lit - tle bit of wine, and we've got a feast in - deed!

Am   D⁷   G   A⁷(–) D⁷   G

2. We don't need a fancy menu,
   just the basic things will do;
   Jesus gives us love for sharing
   and he says to me and you:

3. Jesus gave himself for others
   when he died to set us free.
   Now he leads the celebration,
   he's alive in you and me!

Words: Michael Forster
Music: Christopher Tambling

121 Jesus had all kinds of friends

Moderately
Refrain

Je - sus had all kinds of friends, so the gos - pel sto - ries say.

C   G⁷   C   Am   Dm   G⁷   C   G⁷

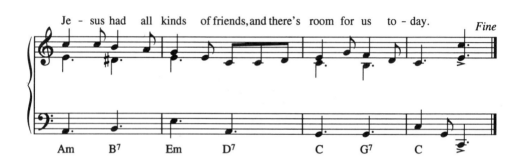

Je - sus had all kinds of friends, and there's room for us to - day.   *Fine*

Am   B⁷   Em   D⁷   C   G⁷   C

1. Some were hap-py, some were sad, some were good and some were bad,

F (Dm)   G⁷   C   Am   Dm   G⁷   C

some were short and some were tall, Je - sus said he loved them all.   *D.C.*

D⁷   G   Em   Am   D⁷   G   G⁷ (G)

2. Some were humble, some were proud,
   some were quiet, some were loud,
   some were fit and some were lame,
   Jesus loved them all the same.

3. Some were healthy, some were sick,
   some were slow and some were quick,
   some were clever, some were not,
   Jesus said he loved the lot!

Words: Michael Forster
Music: Christopher Tambling

122 Jesus is greater

Je - sus is great - er than the great - est he - roes,

Capo 5 C   Am   Dm   G⁷

Je - sus is clo - ser than the clo - sest friends.

C   Am   Dm   G⁷

He came from hea - ven and he died to save us, to

C   Am   Dm   G⁷

show us love that ne - ver ends.

1.   D.C.

F (Dm)   G⁷   C

Words: Gill Hutchinson
Music: Gill Hutchinson, arr. Noel Rawsthorne

123 Jesus' love is very wonderful

Words: H.W. Rattle
Music: unknown, arr. Noel Rawsthorne

124 Jesus put this song into our hearts

'Hebrew' style, getting faster

Each verse should be sung faster

Jesus taught us how to live in harmony,
Jesus taught us how to live in harmony;
diff'rent faces, diff'rent races, he made us one.
Jesus taught us how to live in harmony.

3. Jesus turned our sorrow into dancing,
Jesus turned our sorrow into dancing;
changed our tears of sadness into rivers of joy.
Jesus turned our sorrow into a dance.

Words: Words: Graham Kendrick
Music: Graham Kendrick, arr. Christopher Tambling

125 Jesus, remember me

Words: Luke 23:42
Music: Jacques Berthier

126 Jesus took a piece of bread

2. We share with one another
    the bread and wine he gives,
    and celebrate together
    the special life he lives.

3. We rise up from the table,
    and go where Jesus sends,
    to tell the world the gospel
    of love that never ends.

Words: Michael Forster
Music: traditional English melody, arr. Alan Ridout

127 Jesus went away to the desert
Ain't listenin' to no temptation

1. Je - sus went a - way to the de - sert, pray - ing,

D   B7   Em   A7

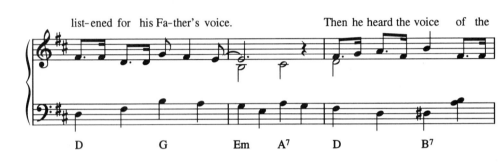

list - ened for his Fa - ther's voice.   Then he heard the voice   of the

D   G   Em   A7   D   B7

temp - ter say - ing, 'Why not make the ea - sy choice?'

Em   A7   D   Bm (D)   E7   A

Refrain

Ain't lis - t'nin' to   no temp - ta - tion,   ain't fall - in' for

D   F(Dm)

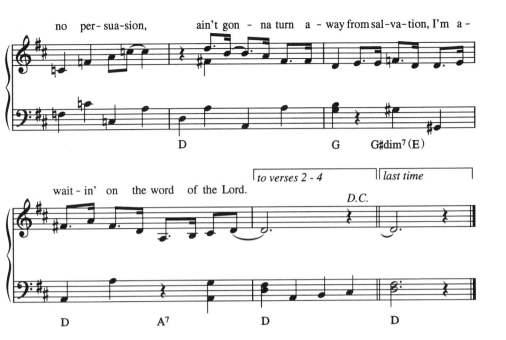

2. 'There's an easy way if you'd only choose it,
   you can turn the stones to bread!
   What's the good of pow'r if you don't abuse it?
   Gotta keep yourself well fed!'

3. 'What about a stunt to attract attention,
   showing off your special pow'r?
   You'd get more applause than I'd care to mention
   jumping from the Temple tow'r!'

4. 'Ev'rything you want will be right there for you,
   listen to the words I say!
   Nobody who matters will dare ignore you;
   my way is the easy way.'

Words: Michael Forster
Music: Christopher Tambling

The
Children's
Hymn
Book

128 Jesus will never, ever

Words: Greg Leavers
Music: Greg Leavers, arr. Noel Rawsthorne

129 Jesus, you love me

With feeling

Words and Music: David Hind

130 Jubilate, everybody

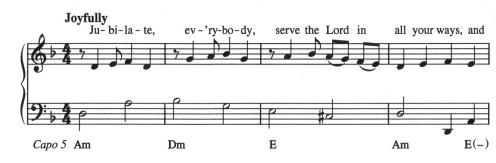

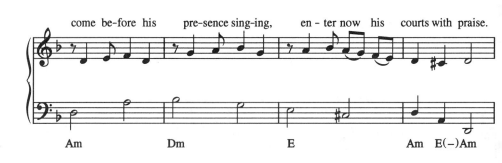

Words: Fred Dunn
Music: Fred Dunn, arr. Christopher Tambling

131 Just imagine

1. Just i-ma-gine hav-ing a world where peo-ple care,

G Am D   C Am Dsus⁴(D) D

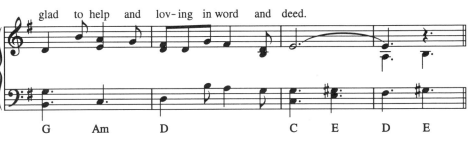

glad to help and lov-ing in word and deed.

G Am D   C E D E

Refrain

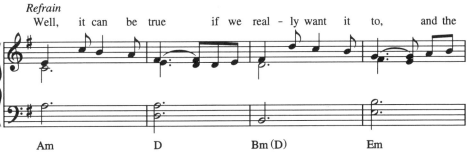

Well, it can be true if we real-ly want it to, and the

Am D   Bm(D) Em

love of Je-sus liv-ing in us is all we need.

Am G   D⁷ G

2. Just imagine having a world
   where people care,
   glad to give
   without any hate or greed.

Words: Susan Sayers
Music: Susan Sayers, arr. Noel Rawsthorne

132 King of kings

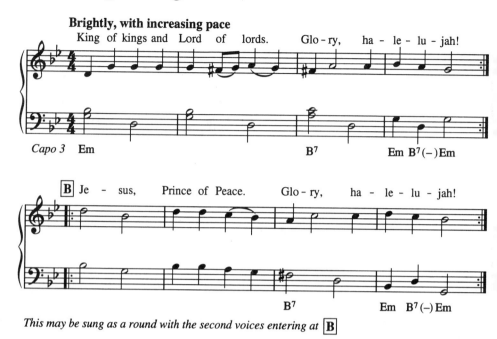

This may be sung as a round with the second voices entering at **B**

Words: Sophie Conty and Naomi Batya
Music: Sophie Conty and Naomi Batya, arr. Christopher Tambling

133 Kum ba yah

1. Kum ba yah, my Lord, kum ba yah, kum ba yah, my Lord, kum ba

yah, kum ba yah, my Lord, kum ba yah, O Lord, kum ba yah.

2. Someone's crying, Lord, kum ba yah,
   someone's crying, Lord, kum ba yah,
   someone's crying, Lord, kum ba yah,
   O Lord, kum ba yah.

3. Someone's singing, Lord, kum ba yah,
   someone's singing, Lord, kum ba yah,
   someone's singing, Lord, kum ba yah,
   O Lord, kum ba yah.

4. Someone's praying, Lord, kum ba yah,
   someone's praying, Lord, kum ba yah,
   someone's praying, Lord, kum ba yah,
   O Lord, kum ba yah.

Words: Spiritual
Music: Spiritual, arr. Alan Ridout

134 Kyrie eleison

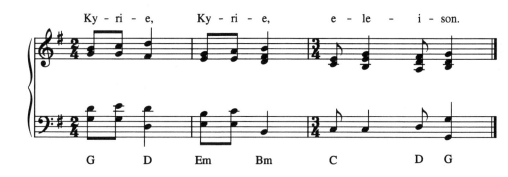

'Kyrie, eleison' is Greek and means 'Lord, have mercy.'

Words: traditional
Music: Jacques Berthier

135 Lamb of God

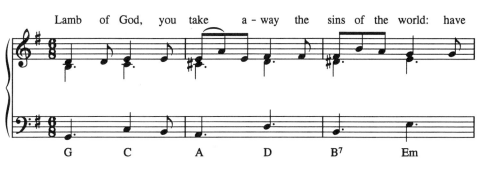

Lamb of God, you take a-way the sins of the world: have

G C A D B⁷ Em

mer-cy on us, have mer-cy on us. Lamb of God, you

C G C D(−) G G C

take a-way the sins of the world: grant us

A D B⁷ Em Am

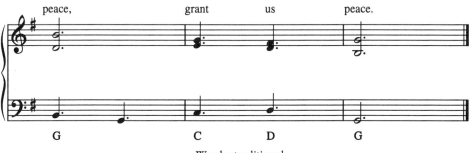

peace, grant us peace.

G C D G

Words: traditional
Music: Gerry Fitzpatrick, arr. Norman Warren

136 Laudato sii

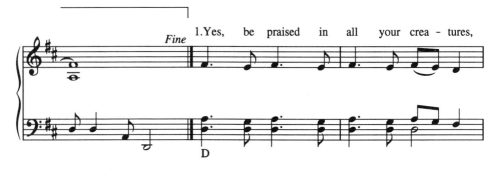

sun our bro - ther, moon our sis - ter, in the stars and

Bm (D)　　　　　　　　　　G

in the bree - zes, air and fire and flow - ing wa - ter.　*D.C.*

A⁷

2. Thank you for the earth, our mother,
   she who feeds us and sustains us;
   for her fruits, her grass, her flowers,
   for the mountains and the oceans.

3. Praise for those who spread forgiveness,
   those who share your peace with others,
   bearing trials and sickness bravely.
   Even sister death won't harm them.

4. Life is but a song of worship,
   and the reason for our singing
   is to praise you for the music,
   join the dance of all creation!

5. Praise to you, our God and Father,
   praise and thanks to you, Lord Jesus,
   praise to you, most Holy Spirit,
   life and joy of all creation!

'Laudato sii, O mi Signore' is Italian and means 'Praise be to you, O my Lord'.

Words: Damian Lundy, after St Francis of Assisi
Music: traditional Italian melody, arr. Norman Warren

137 Let love be real

Slowly, with expression

1. Let love be real, in giv-ing and re-ceiv-ing, with-out the

Capo 3   A⁷   D   G   A⁷

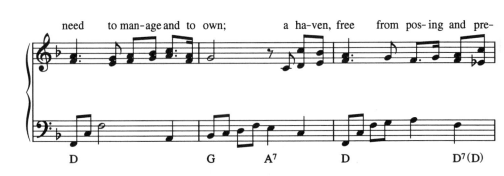

need to man-age and to own; a ha-ven, free from pos-ing and pre-

D   G   A⁷   D   D⁷ (D)

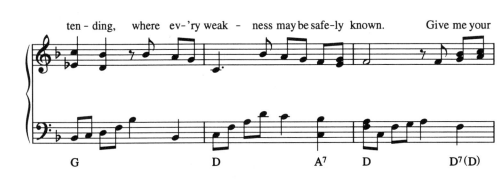

ten-ding, where ev-'ry weak-ness may be safe-ly known. Give me your

G   D   A⁷   D   D⁷ (D)

hand, a-long the de-sert path-way, give me your love wher-e-ver we may

G   D   Em

2. Let love be real, not grasping or confining,
   that strange embrace that holds yet sets us free;
   that helps us face the risk of truly living,
   and makes us brave to be what we might be.
   Give me your strength when all my words are weakness;
   give me your love in spite of all you know.
   Still be my friend, my critic and my lover.
   Don't make me change,
   don't make me strange,
   but let me grow.

3. Let love be real, with no manipulation,
   no secret wish to harness or control;
   let us accept each other's incompleteness,
   and share the joy of learning to be whole.
   Give me your hope through dreams and disappointments;
   give me your trust when all my failings show.
   Still be my friend, my critic and my lover.
   Don't make me change,
   don't make me strange,
   but let me grow.

Words: Michael Forster
Music: Christopher Tambling

138 Let the mountains dance and sing

2. Let the water sing its song!
   And the pow'rful wind so strong
   whistle as it blows along!
   Alleluia!

3. Let the blossom all break out
   in a huge unspoken shout,
   just to show that God's about!
   Alleluia!

Words: Susan Sayers
Music: Susan Sayers, arr. Noel Rawsthorne

139 Let us talents and tongues employ

2. Christ is able to make us one,
   at the table he sets the tone,
   teaching people to live to bless,
   love in word and in deed express.

3. Jesus calls us in, sends us out
   bearing fruit in a world of doubt,
   gives us love to tell, bread to share:
   God-Immanuel ev'rywhere!

Words: Fred Kaan
Music: traditional Jamaican melody adapted by Doreen Potter, arr. Noel Rawsthorne

140 Life for the poor was hard and tough
Jesus turned the water into wine

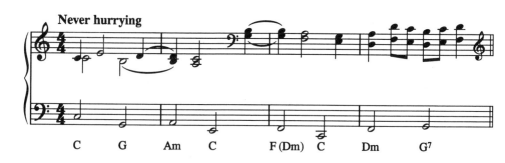

Never hurrying

C G Am C F (Dm) C Dm G⁷

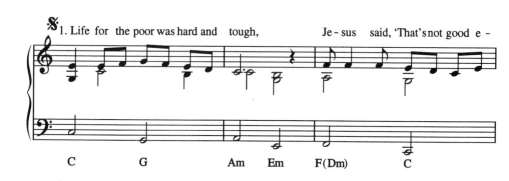

1. Life for the poor was hard and tough, Je-sus said, 'That's not good e-

C G Am Em F(Dm) C

nough; life should be great and here's the sign:

Dm G⁷ C G Am Em

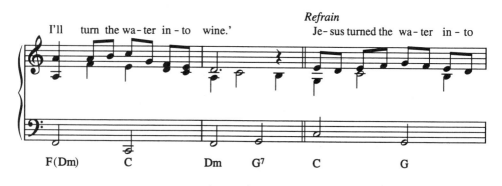

I'll turn the wa-ter in-to wine.' *Refrain* Je-sus turned the wa-ter in-to

F(Dm) C Dm G⁷ C G

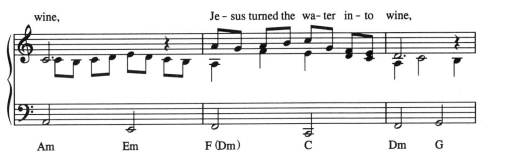

wine,   Je - sus turned the wa- ter in - to wine,

Am   Em   F (Dm)   C   Dm   G

Je- sus turned the wa- ter in - to wine,   and the peo - ple saw that

C   G   Am   Em   Dm   C

life   was   good.

Dm   G⁷   C   G   Am   Em

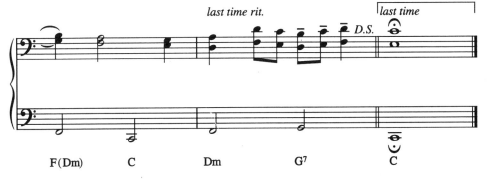

last time rit.   *last time*   D.S.

F (Dm)   C   Dm   G⁷   C

2. Life is a thing to be enjoyed,
   not to be wasted or destroyed.
   Laughter is part of God's design;
   let's turn the water into wine!

3. Go to the lonely and the sad,
   give them the news to make them glad,
   helping the light of hope to shine,
   turning the water into wine!

Words: Michael Forster
Music: Christopher Tambling

The
Children's
Hymn
Book

141 Life is for living now

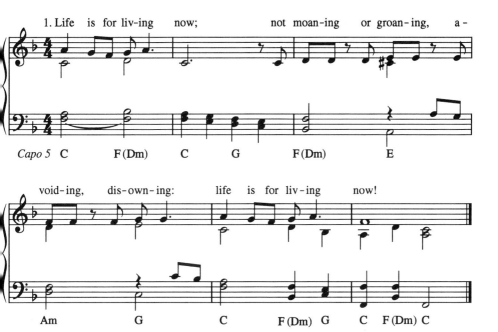

2. Life is for living now;
   not killing or caging,
   destroying or grasping:
   life is for living now!

3. Life is for living now;
   for feeling and thinking,
   for growing and finding:
   life is for living now!

4. Life is for living now;
   for praying and serving,
   for living and loving:
   life is for living now!

5. Life is for living now;
   for healing and freeing,
   rejoicing and dancing:
   life is for living now!

Words: W.L. Wallace
Music: Andrew Moore

142 Listen, let your heart keep seeking

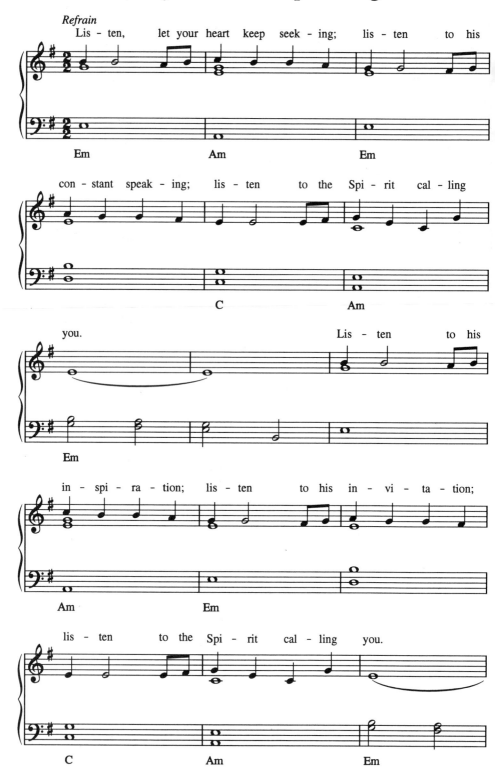

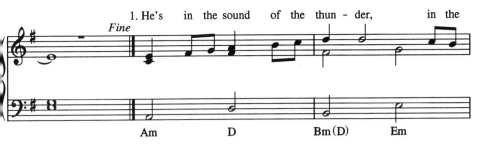

1. He's in the sound of the thun-der, in the

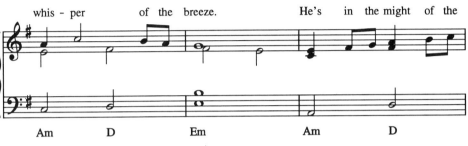

whis-per of the breeze. He's in the might of the

whirl-wind, in the roar-ing of the seas.

2. He's in the laughter of children,
   in the patter of the rain.
   Hear him in cries of the suff'ring,
   in their sorrow and their pain.

3. He's in the noise of the city,
   in the singing of the birds.
   And in the night time, the stillness
   helps you listen to his word.

Words: Aniceto Nazareth
Music: Aniceto Nazareth, arr. Noel Rawsthorne

143 Lord, have mercy

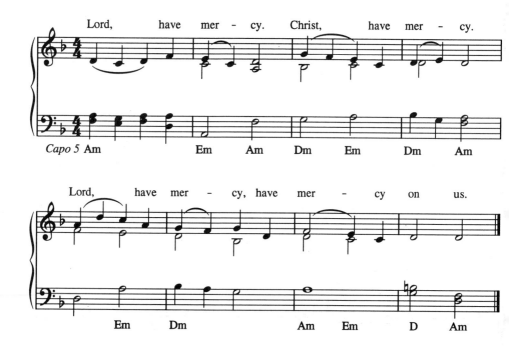

Words: traditional
Music: Colin Mawby

144 Lord, have mercy on us
Kyrie

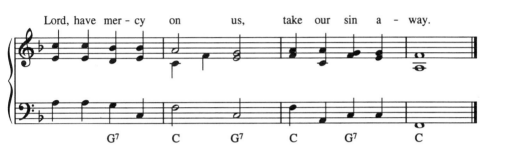

2. Christ, have mercy on us,
   hear us as we pray;
   Christ, have mercy on us,
   take our sin away.

3. Lord, have mercy on us,
   hear us as we pray;
   Lord, have mercy on us,
   take our sin away.

Words: Michael Forster
Music: Friedrich Filitz, arr. Norman Warren

145 Lord Jesus Christ
Living Lord

2. Lord Jesus Christ,
   now and ev'ry day
   teach us how to pray,
   Son of God.
   You have commanded us to do
   this in remembrance, Lord, of you,
   into our lives your pow'r breaks through,
   living Lord.

3. Lord Jesus Christ,
   you have come to us,
   born as one of us,
   Mary's Son.
   Led out to die on Calvary,
   risen from death to set us free,
   living Lord Jesus, help us see
   you are Lord.

4. Lord Jesus Christ,
   I would come to you,
   live my life for you,
   Son of God.
   All your commands I know are true,
   your many gifts will make me new,
   into my life your pow'r breaks through,
   living Lord.

Verse 2 is suitable for Communion.

Words: Patrick Appleford
Music: Patrick Appleford, arr. Noel Rawsthorne

146 Lord of all hopefulness

1. Lord of all hope-ful-ness, Lord of all joy, whose trust, e - ver

Capo 1   D   G   D   A

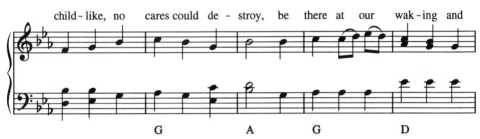

child - like, no cares could de - stroy, be there at our wak-ing and

G   A   G   D

give us, we pray, your bliss in our hearts, Lord, at the break of the day.

G   D   Bm (D)   G   D

2. Lord of all eagerness,
   Lord of all faith,
   whose strong hands were skilled
   at the plane and the lathe,
   be there at our labours
   and give us, we pray,
   your strength in our hearts, Lord,
   at the noon of the day.

3. Lord of all kindliness,
   Lord of all grace,
   your hands swift to welcome,
   your arms to embrace,
   be there at our homing
   and give us, we pray,
   your love in our hearts, Lord,
   at the eve of the day.

4. Lord of all gentleness,
   Lord of all calm,
   whose voice is contentment,
   whose presence is balm,
   be there at our sleeping
   and give us, we pray,
   your peace in our hearts, Lord,
   at the end of the day.

Words: Jan Struther
Music: traditional Irish melody, arr. Alan Ridout

147 Lord of the future

2. Lord of tomorrow,
   Lord of today,
   Lord over all, you are worthy.
   Lord of creation,
   Lord of all truth,
   we give all praise to you.

Words: Ian D. Craig
Music: Ian D. Craig, arr. Noel Rawsthorne

148 Lord, the light of your love
Shine, Jesus, shine

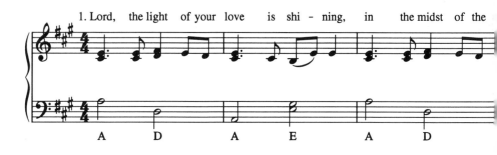

1. Lord, the light of your love is shi-ning, in the midst of the

A   D   A   E   A   D

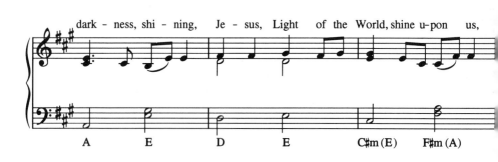

dark-ness, shi-ning, Je-sus, Light of the World, shine u-pon us,

A   E   D   E   C#m(E)   F#m(A)

set us free by the truth you now bring us, shine on me,

D   E7   C#m(E)   F#m(A)   G   Esus4(E) E

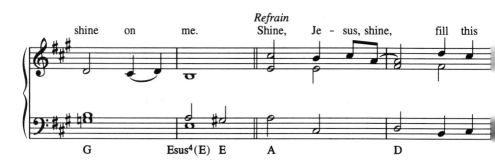

shine on me.   *Refrain*   Shine, Je-sus, shine, fill this

G   Esus4(E) E   A   D

land with the Fa-ther's glo-ry, blaze, Spi-rit, blaze,

Bm(D)　　　E　　　A

set our hearts on fire. Flow, ri-ver, flow,

D　　Bm(D)　G　E　A

flood the na-tions with grace and mer-cy; send forth your word,

D　　Bm(D)　　E　　A

Lord, and let there be light!

to verses 2 & 3　last time
D.C.

D　　Bm(D)　E　A　D　A　D　A

Lord, I come to your awesome presence,
from the shadows into your radiance;
by the blood I may enter your brightness,
search me, try me, consume all my darkness.
Shine on me, shine on me.

3. As we gaze on your kingly brightness,
so our faces display your likeness,
ever changing from glory to glory,
mirrored here, may our lives tell your story.
Shine on me, shine on me.

Words: Graham Kendrick
Music: Graham Kendrick, arr. Christopher Tambling

The
Children's
Hymn
Book

149 Lord, we've come to worship you

With a gentle rhythm

Lord, we've come to wor-ship you, Lord, we've come to praise; Lord, we've come to wor-ship you in oh so ma-ny ways. Some of us shout and some of us sing, and some of us whis-per the praise we bring, but, Lord, we all are ga-ther-ing to give to you our praise.

Words: Ian Smale
Music: Ian Smale, arr. Noel Rawsthorne

150 Lord, you've promised through your Son
Lord, forgive us

© Copyright 1992 Daybreak Music Ltd, Silverdale Road, Eastbourne, East Sussex BN20 7AB.
Used by permission.

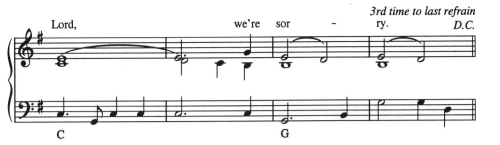

3rd time to last refrain
D.C.

Lord, we're sor - ry.

C   G

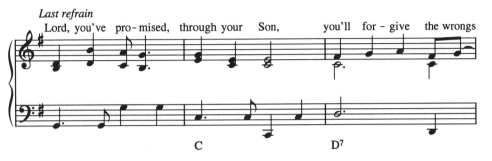

Last refrain
Lord, you've pro-mised, through your Son, you'll for - give the wrongs

C   D⁷

we've done; we re - ceive your par - don,

G   G⁷   C

Lord, as you for - give us.

D⁷   G   C   G

2. Sinful and unkind thoughts too,
all of these are known to you.
Lord, we're sorry.
Lord, we're sorry.

3. And the things we've left undone,
words and deeds we should have done.
Lord, we're sorry.
Lord, we're sorry.

Last refrain:
Lord, you've promised, through your Son,
you'll forgive the wrong we've done;
we receive your pardon,
Lord, as you forgive us.

Words: Alan J. Price
Music: Alan J. Price, arr. Norman Warren

151 Love is like a circle

Jauntily

Refrain

Love is * like a cir - cle, * we can join it * a - ny-where. * Let's

C A⁷ Dm G C F (Dm) G

take our cou-rage in our hands and lay a - side des - pair. *Fine*

C F (Dm) G C G⁷ C

1. Some-times it's our neigh-bour, * some-times those at play, *

G D⁷ G D⁷ G D⁷ G

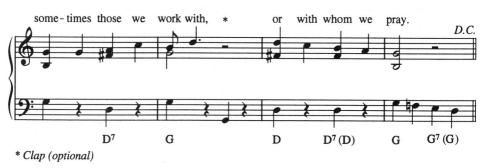

some-times those we work with, * or with whom we pray. *D.C.*

D⁷ G D D⁷ (D) G G⁷ (G)

* *Clap (optional)*

2. Sometimes it's a granny,
   mother or a dad,
   sometimes it's a baby,
   smiling or so sad.

3. Love can come from adults
   and from girls and boys;
   love can come in silence
   or within the noise.

4. Some find love through list'ning,
   some through ardent prayer,
   others in the scriptures,
   some through tender care.

5. Love can make us happy,
   love can bring us tears,
   love can make us peaceful,
   casting out our fears

Last refrain:
   But in all our loving,
   from beginning to the end,
   the love we share all comes from God
   who greets us in each friend.

Words: W.L. Wallace
Music: Martin Setchell

152 Make me a channel of your peace

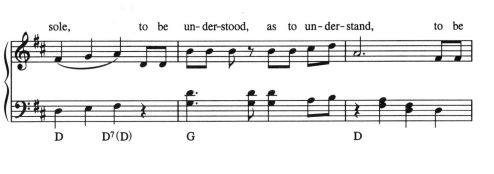

sole,   to be un-der-stood,   as to un-der-stand,   to be

D   D⁷(D)   G   D

loved, as to love with all my soul.   4. Make me a chan-nel of your

E   A   A⁷(A)   D

peace.   It   is   in par-don-ing that we are

par-doned,   in giv-ing of our-selves that we re-

A⁷

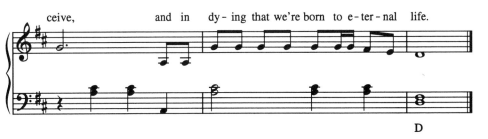

ceive,   and in dy-ing that we're born to e-ter-nal life.

D

Words: Sebastian Temple, based on the Prayer of St Frances of Assisi
Music: Sebastian Temple, arr. Alan Ridout

153 Morning has broken

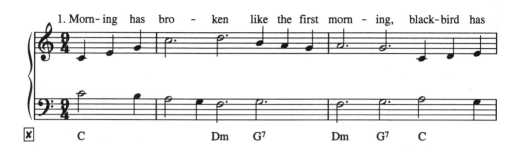

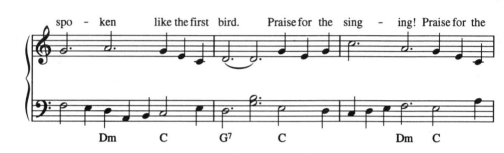

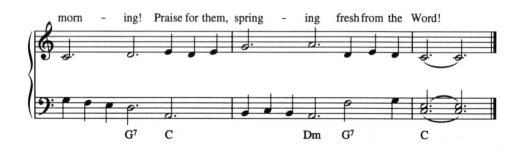

2. Sweet the rain's new fall,
sunlit from heaven,
like the first dew-fall
on the first grass.
Praise for the sweetness
of the wet garden,
sprung in completeness
where his feet pass.

3. Mine is the sunlight!
Mine is the morning,
born of the one light
Eden saw play.
Praise with elation,
praise ev'ry morning,
God's re-creation
of the new day!

Words: Eleanor Farjeon
Music: traditional Irish melody, arr. Alan Ridout

154 My mouth was made for worship

2. My heart was made for loving,
   my mind to know God's ways,
   my body was made a temple,
   my life is one of praise to Jesus.
   And all God's people said: Amen,
   hallelujah, amen, praise and glory,
   amen, amen, amen, amen.
   Wo, wo, wo, wo, wo.

Words: Ian Smale
Music: Ian Smale, arr. Norman Warren

155 Never let Jesus

1. Ne-ver let Jesus in-to your heart un-less you are pre-pared for

Capo 3 D   A⁷   D   G   A⁷

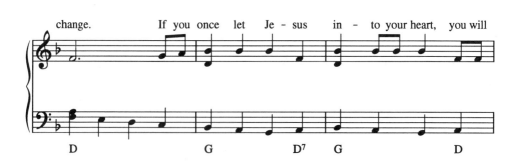

change. If you once let Jesus in-to your heart, you will

D   G   D⁷   G   D

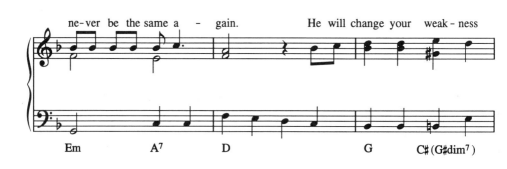

ne-ver be the same a - gain.   He will change your weak-ness

Em   A⁷   D   G   C♯ (G♯dim⁷)

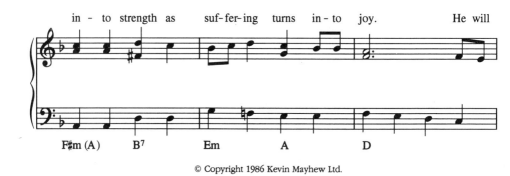

in - to strength as suf-fer-ing turns in-to joy.   He will

F♯m (A)   B⁷   Em   A   D

wash you clean as the drift-ing snow, give peace that no-one can de - stroy

G   A⁷   D   Bm (D)   G   A⁷   D

2. Never let Jesus into your heart
   unless you are prepared for change.
   If you once let Jesus into your heart,
   you will never be the same again.
   He will use your gifts to help this world,
   put you where he needs you to be,
   at the end of time he will welcome you,
   and love you for eternity.

Words: Susan Sayers
Music: Susan Sayers, arr. Noel Rawsthorne

156 Nobody's a nobody

1. No - bo - dy's a no - bo - dy, be - lieve me 'cause it's true.

Capo 1 E   A   B⁷

No - bo - dy's a no - bo - dy, es - pe - cial - ly not you.

E

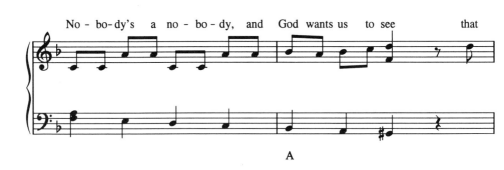

No - bo - dy's a no - bo - dy, and God wants us to see   that

A

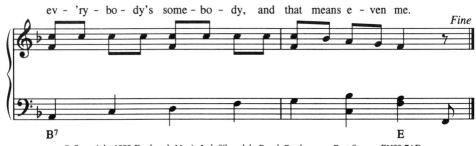

ev - 'ry - bo - dy's some - bo - dy, and that means e - ven me.

Fine

B⁷   E

2. I'm no car-toon, I'm hu-man, I have feel-ings, treat me right. I'm

A   B⁷

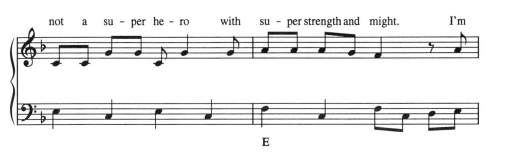

not a su-per he-ro with su-per strength and might. I'm

E

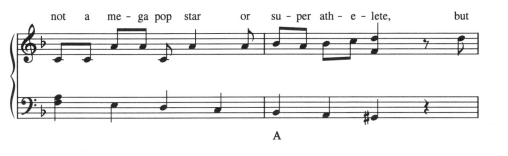

not a me-ga pop star or su-per ath-e-lete, but

A

did you know I'm spec-ial in fact I'm quite u-nique!

D.C.

B⁷   E

Words: John Hardwick
Music: John Hardwick, arr. Noel Rawsthorne

157 Not every day

Allegretto dolce

1. Not ev - 'ry day shall

earth's bright rain-bow co - lours arch o-ver clear and spark-ling az - ure skies;

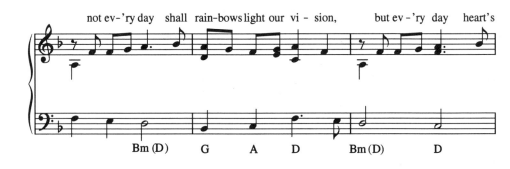

not ev-'ry day shall rain-bows light our vi - sion, but ev-'ry day heart's

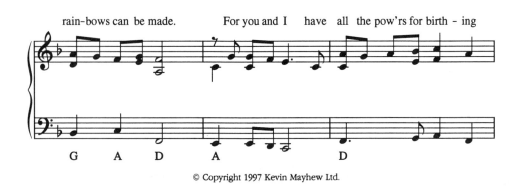

rain-bows can be made. For you and I have all the pow'rs for birth - ing

a rain-bow bright, with - in our hearts and minds; yes, with new thoughts and

through new ways of see - ing, our lives can span the hues of tech-ni-col-our light.

2. On ev'ry day a heaven lies within us,
   awaiting space within our hearts and thoughts;
   on ev'ry day, a peace can flood our thinking,
   when we let go of clutter in the mind.
   Within the space of letting go of all things,
   the God of wholeness heals our brokenness,
   and we are one with all that seemed divided:
   a home of love where ev'ry fractured mind can rest.

Words: W.L. Wallace
Music: Andrew Gant

158 O give thanks

Words: Joanne Pond
Music: Joanne Pond, arr. Noel Rawsthorne

159 O Lamb of God

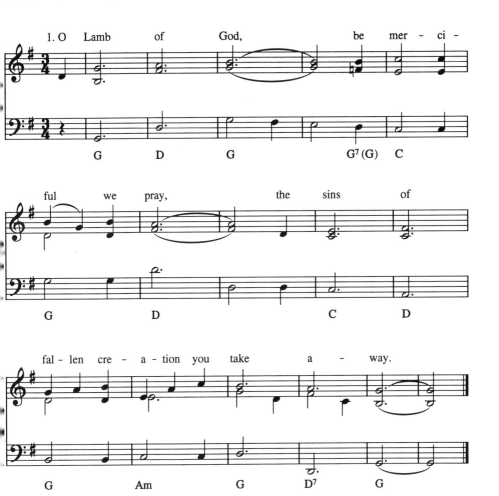

2. O Lamb of God, you bear creation's pain.
   Have mercy on us, and cleanse us of ev'ry stain.

3. O Lamb of God, renew the life of earth,
   and by your Spirit bring justice and peace to birth.

Words: Michael Forster
Music: traditional melody, arr. Norman Warren

Text and this arrangement © Copyright 1995 Kevin Mayhew Ltd.

160 O Lamb of God, you cleanse our hearts

1. O Lamb of God, you cleanse our hearts and take our sin a-

way. O Lamb of God, your grace im - part, and

let our gui - lty fear de - part, have mer - cy, Lord, we

pray, have mer - cy, Lord, we pray.

2. O Lamb of God, our lives restore,
   our guilty souls release.
   Into our lives your Spirit pour
   and let us live for evermore
   in perfect heav'nly peace,
   in perfect heav'nly peace.

Words: Michael Forster
Music: Hubert Parry, arr. Alan Ridout

161 O Lord all the world belongs to you

2. The world's only loving to its friends,
   but you have brought us love that never ends;
   loving enemies too,
   and this loving with you
   is what's turning the world upside down.

3. This world lives divided and apart.
   You draw us all together and we start,
   in your body, to see
   that in fellowship we
   can be turning the world upside down.

4. The world wants the wealth to live in state,
   but you show us a new way to be great:
   like a servant you came,
   and if we do the same,
   we'll be turning the world upside down.

5. O Lord, all the world belongs to you,
   and you are always making all things new.
   Send your Spirit on all
   in your church, whom you call
   to be turning the world upside down.

Words: Patrick Appleford,
Music: Patrick Appleford, arr. Noel Rawsthorne

162 O Lord, hear my prayer

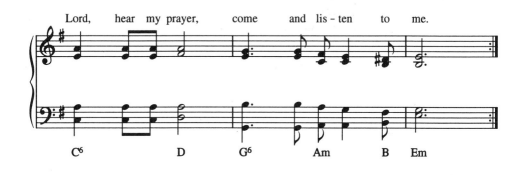

Words: Taizé Community
Music: Jacques Berthier

163 O when the saints go marching in

2. O when they crown him Lord of all,
   O when they crown him Lord of all,
   I want to be in that number
   when they crown him Lord of all.

3. O when all knees bow at his name,
   O when all knees bow at his name,
   I want to be in that number
   when all knees bow at his name.

4. O when they sing the Saviour's praise,
   O when they sing the Saviour's praise,
   I want to be in that number
   when they sing the Saviour's praise.

5. O when the saints go marching in,
   O when the saints go marching in,
   I want to be in that number
   when the saints go marching in.

Words: traditional
Music: traditional, arr. Noel Rawsthorne

164 Oh! Oh! Oh! how good is the Lord

With a swing

Refrain

Oh! Oh! Oh! how good is the Lord, Oh! Oh! Oh! how good is the Lord,

Capo 5 G   Am   D⁷   G

Oh! Oh! Oh! how good is the Lord, I ne-ver will for-get what he has

G⁷ (G)   C   D

done for me. *Fine* 1. He gives me sal-va-tion, how good is the Lord, he

G   D⁷   G   Am

gives me sal-va-tion, how good is the Lord, he gives me sal-va-tion, how

D⁷   G   G⁷ (G)

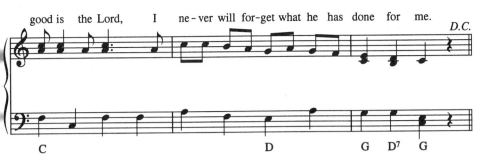

2. He gives me his blessings, how good is the Lord,
   he gives me his blessings, how good is the Lord,
   he gives me his blessings, how good is the Lord,
   I never will forget what he has done for me.

3. He gives me his Spirit, how good is the Lord,
   he gives me his Spirit, how good is the Lord,
   he gives me his Spirit, how good is the Lord,
   I never will forget what he has done for me.

4. He gives me his healing, how good is the Lord,
   he gives me his healing, how good is the Lord,
   he gives me his healing, how good is the Lord,
   I never will forget what he has done for me.

5. He gives me his glory, how good is the Lord,
   he gives me his glory, how good is the Lord,
   he gives me his glory, how good is the Lord,
   I never will forget what he has done for me.

Other verses may be added as appropriate.

Words: unknown
Music: unknown, arr. Noel Rawsthorne

165 One hundred and fifty-three!

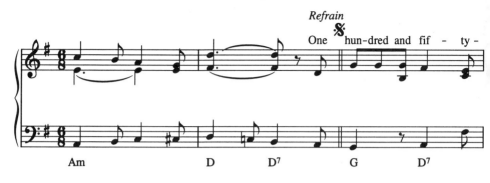

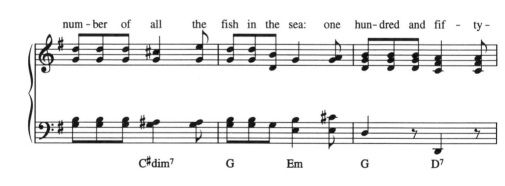

Je - sus said, 'Try once more.' So we doubt-ful - ly tried on the

Am   B⁷   Em   Am   D

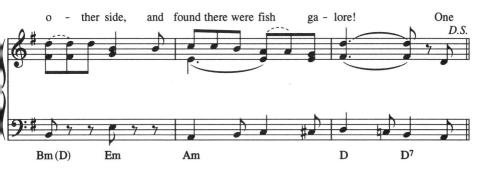

o - ther side, and found there were fish ga - lore! One

D.S.

Bm (D)   Em   Am   D   D⁷

2. We got all the fish to the shore,
   we wondered how many there'd be.
   So we started to count,
   and what an amount:
   one hundred and fifty-three!

3. Now here was a wonderful sight
   we'd never expected to see;
   and the net didn't break,
   it was able to take
   the hundred and fifty-three!

4. So whether you're rich or you're poor,
   whatever your race or your sect,
   be you black, white or brown,
   Jesus wants you around,
   there's plenty of room in the net!

Words: Michael Forster
Music: Christopher Tambling

166 One more step along the world I go

1. One more step a-long the world I go, one more step a-long the

G   D   D⁷(D)

world I go. From the old things to the new

G   C   G

keep me tra-vel-ling a-long with you. *Refrain* And it's from the old I

D⁷   G   C

tra-vel to the new, keep me tra-vel-ling a-long with you.

D⁷   G   D⁷   G

2. Round the corners of the world I turn,
    more and more about the world I learn.
    All the new things that I see
    you'll be looking at along with me.

3. As I travel through the bad and good,
    keep me travelling the way I should.
    Where I see no way to go
    you'll be telling me the way, I know.

4. Give me courage when the world is rough,
    keep me loving though the world is tough.
    Leap and sing in all I do,
    keep me travelling along with you.

5. You are older than the world can be,
    you are younger than the life in me.
    Ever old and ever new,
    keep me travelling along with you.

Words: Sydney Carter
Music: Sydney Carter, arr. Noel Rawsthorne

167 Our Father
Caribbean Lord's Prayer

2. On earth as it is in heaven,
   hallowèd be thy name.
   Give us this day our daily bread,
   hallowèd be thy name,
   hallowèd be thy name.

3. Forgive us our trespasses,
   hallowèd be thy name.
   As we forgive those who trespass against us.
   hallowèd be thy name,
   hallowèd be thy name.

4. Lead us not into temptation,
   hallowèd be thy name.
   But deliver us from all that is evil,
   hallowèd be thy name,
   hallowèd be thy name.

5. For thine is the kingdom, the pow'r and the glory,
   hallowèd be thy name.
   For ever and for ever and ever,
   hallowèd be thy name,
   hallowèd be thy name.

6. Amen, amen, it shall be so,
   hallowèd be thy name.
   Amen, amen, it shall be so,
   hallowèd be thy name,
   hallowèd be thy name.

Words: Mathew 6:9-13 and Luke 11:2-4
Music: traditional Caribbean, arr. Noel Rawsthorne

168 Our Father

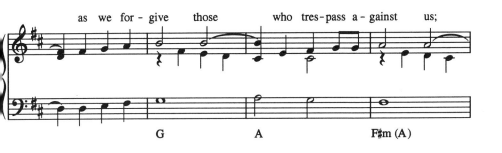

as we for-give those who tres-pass a-gainst us;

G   A   F♯m (A)

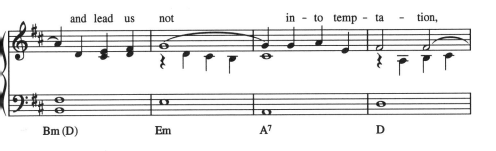

and lead us not in - to temp - ta - tion,

Bm (D)   Em   A⁷   D

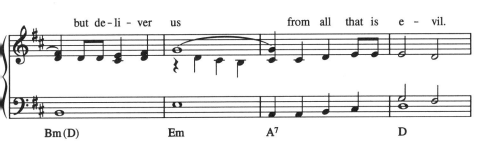

but de-li - ver us from all that is e - vil.

Bm (D)   Em   A⁷   D

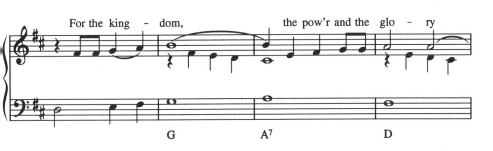

For the king - dom, the pow'r and the glo - ry

G   A⁷   D

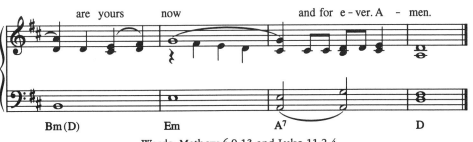

are yours now and for e - ver. A - men.

Bm (D)   Em   A⁷   D

Words: Mathew 6:9-13 and Luke 11:2-4
Music: Julian Wiener, arr. Noel Rawsthorne

169 Our God is so great

Brightly

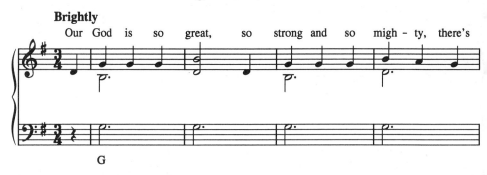

Our God is so great, so strong and so migh-ty, there's

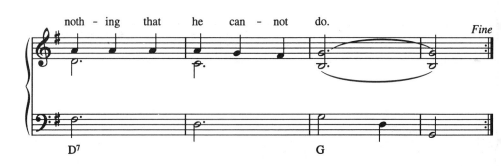

noth-ing that he can-not do. *Fine*

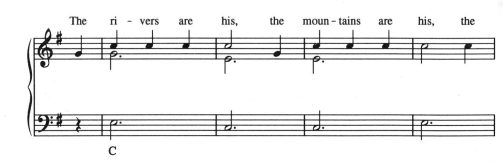

The ri-vers are his, the moun-tains are his, the

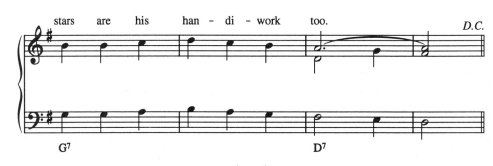

stars are his han-di-work too. *D.C.*

Words: unknown
Music: unknown, arr. John Ballantine

170 Out to the great wide world we go

Joyfully

Refrain

Out to the great wide world we go! Out to the great wide world we go!

C G⁷ C A⁷ Dm G⁷

Out to the great wide world we go and we sing of the love of Je-sus. *Fine*

C C⁷(C) F(Dm) D C G⁷ C

1. Go and tell our neigh-bours, go and tell our friends,

F(Dm) G⁷ C Am Dm G⁷ C G⁷

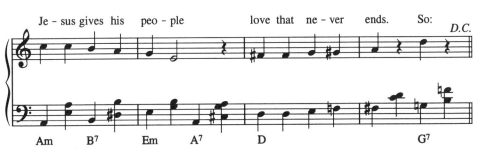

Je-sus gives his peo-ple love that ne-ver ends. So: *D.C.*

Am B⁷ Em A⁷ D G⁷

2. People sad and lonely,
   wond'ring how to cope;
   let's find ways of showing
   Jesus gives us hope. So:

Words: Michael Forster
Music: Christopher Tambling

The
Children's
Hymn
Book

171 Over the earth is a mat of green

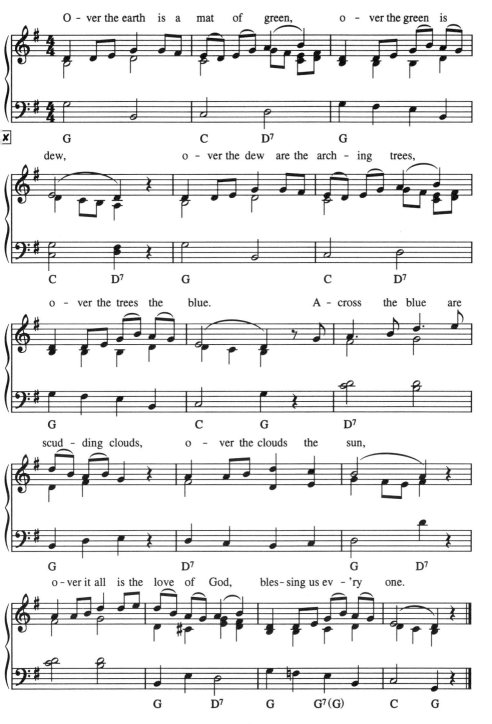

Words: Ruth Brown
Music: traditional Scottish melody arr. Herbert Wiseman, adapted by Guthrie Foote

172 Peace is flowing like a river

This arrangement © Copyright 1997 Kevin Mayhew Ltd.

2. Love is flowing like a river,
   flowing out through you and me,
   spreading out into the desert,
   setting all the captives free.

3. Joy is flowing like a river,
   flowing out through you and me,
   spreading out into the desert,
   setting all the captives free.

4. Faith is flowing like a river,
   flowing out through you and me,
   spreading out into the desert,
   setting all the captives free.

5. Hope is flowing like a river,
   flowing out through you and me,
   spreading out into the desert,
   setting all the captives free.

This version, without the refrain, is popular in many places. It also allows the piece to be sung in a higher key:

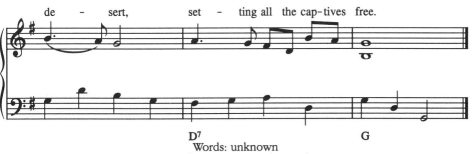

Words: unknown
Music: unknown, arr. Noel Rawsthorne

173 Peace, perfect peace is the gift

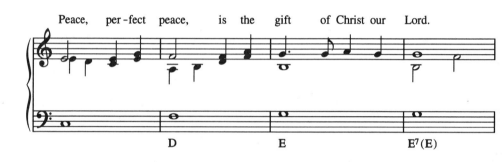

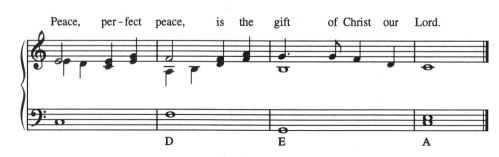

2. Love, perfect love,
   is the gift of Christ our Lord.
   Love, perfect love,
   is the gift of Christ our Lord.
   Thus, says the Lord,
   will the world know my friends.
   Love, perfect love,
   is the gift of Christ our Lord.

3. Faith, perfect faith,
   is the gift of Christ our Lord.
   Faith, perfect faith,
   is the gift of Christ our Lord.
   Thus, says the Lord,
   will the world know my friends.
   Faith, perfect faith,
   is the gift of Christ our Lord.

4. Hope, perfect hope,
   is the gift of Christ our Lord.
   Hope, perfect hope,
   is the gift of Christ our Lord.
   Thus, says the Lord,
   will the world know my friends.
   Hope, perfect hope,
   is the gift of Christ our Lord.

5. Joy, perfect joy,
   is the gift of Christ our Lord.
   Joy, perfect joy,
   is the gift of Christ our Lord.
   Thus, says the Lord,
   will the world know my friends.
   Joy, perfect joy,
   is the gift of Christ our Lord.

Words and Music: Kevin Mayhew

174 Praise and thanksgiving

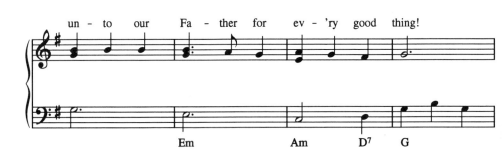

Words: unknown
Music: unknown, arr. Noel Rawsthorne

175 Praise God from whom all blessings flow
Doxology

Praise God from whom all bless - ings flow, praise

Capo 1   D   G   A

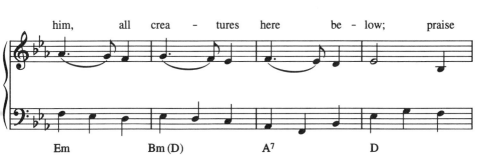

him, all crea - tures here be - low; praise

Em   Bm (D)   A⁷   D

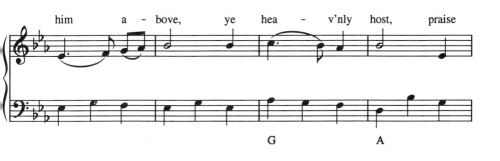

him a - bove, ye hea - v'nly host, praise

G   A

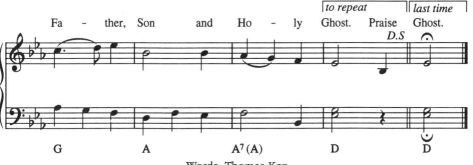

to repeat   *last time*

Fa - ther, Son and Ho - ly Ghost. Praise Ghost.

D.S

G   A   A⁷ (A)   D   D

Words: Thomas Ken
Music: Jimmy Owens, arr. Noel Rawsthorne

176 Praise God in his holy place

2. Praise him with the ol' wood block!
   Let it swing and let it rock,
   praising God around the clock!
   Let ev'rything praise our God!

3. Praise him with the big bass drum,
   if you've got guitars, then strum!
   Now let's make those rafters hum!
   Let ev'rything praise our God!

4. Praise him with the chime bars' chime,
   tell the bells it's party time,
   help those singers find a rhyme!
   Let ev'rything praise our God!

5. Violin or xylophone,
   trumpets with their awesome tone;
   bowed or beaten, bashed or blown,
   let ev'rything praise our God!

6. Cymbals, triangles and things,
   if it crashes, howls or rings,
   ev'rybody shout and sing!
   Let ev'rything praise our God!

Words: Michael Forster
Music: Christopher Tambling

177 Praise him in the morning

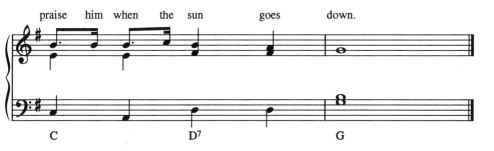

2. Love him, love him,
   love him in the morning,
   love him in the noontime.
   Love him, love him,
   love him when the sun goes down.

3. Trust him, trust him,
   trust him in the morning,
   trust him in the noontime.
   Trust him, trust him,
   trust him when the sun goes down.

4. Serve him, serve him,
   serve him in the morning,
   serve him in the noontime.
   Serve him, serve him,
   serve him when the sun goes down.

5. Jesus, Jesus,
   Jesus in the morning,
   Jesus in the noontime.
   Jesus, Jesus,
   Jesus when the sun goes down.

Words: unknown
Music: unknown, arr. Noel Rawsthorne

178 Push, little seed

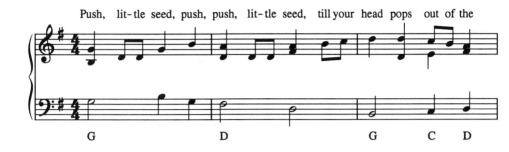

Push, lit-tle seed, push, push, lit-tle seed, till your head pops out of the

ground. This is the air, and now you are there you can

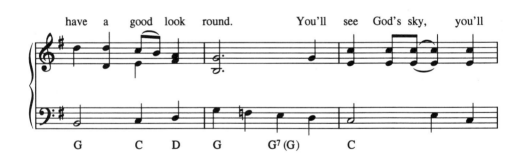

have a good look round. You'll see God's sky, you'll

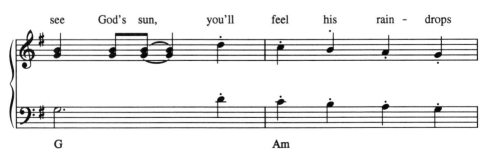

see God's sun, you'll feel his rain - drops

Words: Susan Sayers
Music: Susan Sayers, arr. Noel Rawsthorne

179 Put your trust

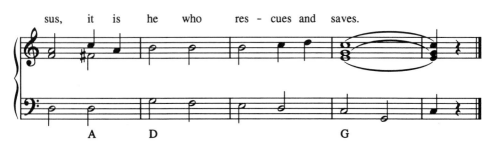

2. Put your trust in the man who cured the blind,
   put your trust in the man who helped the lame,
   put your trust in the Lord Jesus,
   there is healing strength in his name.

3. Put your trust in the man who died for you,
   put your trust in the man who conquered fear,
   put your trust in the Lord Jesus,
   for he rose from death and he's near.

4. Put your trust in the man who understands,
   put your trust in the man who is your friend,
   put your trust in the Lord Jesus,
   who will give you life without end.

Words: Estelle White
Music: Estelle White, arr. Noel Rawsthorne

The
Children's
Hymn
Book

180 Rejoice in the Lord always

This may be sung as a round with the second voices entering at B

Words: Evelyn Tarner, based on Philippians 4:4
Music: Evelyn Tarner, arr. Christopher Tambling

181 Rise and shine

Refrain
Rise and shine, and give God his glo-ry, glo-ry. Rise and shine, and

Capo 3 A   D   A

give God his glo-ry, glo-ry. Rise and shine, and give God his glo-ry, glo-ry,

D   A   D

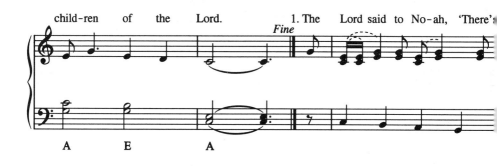

child-ren of the Lord. 1. The Lord said to No-ah, 'There's
Fine

A E A

gon-na be a flood-y, flood-y.' Lord said to No-ah, 'There's

D   A

This arrangement © Copyright 1997 Kevin mayhew Ltd.

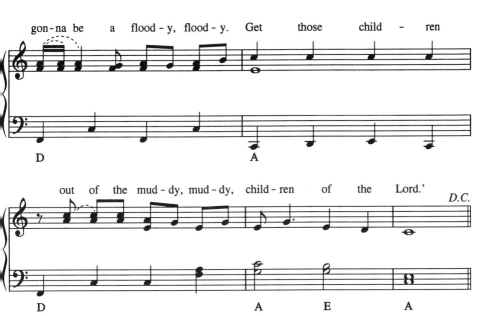

2. So Noah, he built him, he built him an arky, arky,
   Noah, he built him, he built him an arky, arky,
   built it out of hickory barky, barky,
   children of the Lord.

3. The animals, they came on, they came on, by twosies, twosies,
   animals, they came on, they came on, by twosies, twosies,
   elephants and kangaroosies, roosies,
   children of the Lord.

4. It rained and poured for forty daysies, daysies,
   rained and poured for forty daysies, daysies,
   nearly drove those animals crazies, crazies,
   children of the Lord.

5. The sun came out and dried up the landy, landy,
   sun came out and dried up the landy, landy,
   ev'rything was fine and dandy, dandy,
   children of the Lord.

6. If you get to heaven before I do-sies, do-sies,
   you get to heaven before I do-sies, do-sies,
   tell those angels I'm comin' too-sies, too-sies,
   children of the Lord.

Words: unknown, based on Genesis 6:4
Music: traditional, arr. Noel Rawsthorne

182 Said Judas to Mary
Judas and Mary

1. Said Ju-das to Ma-ry, 'Now what will you do with your oint-ment so rich and so
rare?' 'I'll pour it all o-ver the feet of the Lord, and I'll
wipe it a-way with my hair,' she said, 'I'll wipe it a-way with my hair.'

x Capo 3   Em   Bm (D)   Em   Am

B⁷   Em   Bm (D)   Em

Am   D   Em   Bm (D)   C   B⁷   Em

2. 'Oh Mary, oh Mary, oh think of the poor,
this ointment, it could have been sold,
and think of the blankets and think of the bread
you could buy with the silver and gold,' he said,
'you could buy with the silver and gold.'

3. 'Tomorrow, tomorrow, I'll think of the poor,
tomorrow,' she said, 'not today;
for dearer than all of the poor in the world
is my love who is going away,' she said,
'is my love who is going away.'

4. Said Jesus to Mary, 'Your love is so deep,
   today you may do as you will.
   Tomorrow you say I am going away,
   but my body I leave with you still,' he said,
   'my body I leave with you still.'

5. 'The poor of the world are my body,' he said,
   'to the end of the world they shall be.
   The bread and the blankets you give to the poor
   you'll know you have given to me,' he said,
   'you'll know you have given to me.'

6. 'My body will hang on the cross of the world,
   tomorrow,' he said, 'and today,
   and Martha and Mary will find me again
   and wash all my sorrow away,' he said,
   'and wash all my sorrow away.'

Words: Sydney Carter
Music: Sydney Carter, arr. Noel Rawsthorne

183 Save us, O Lord

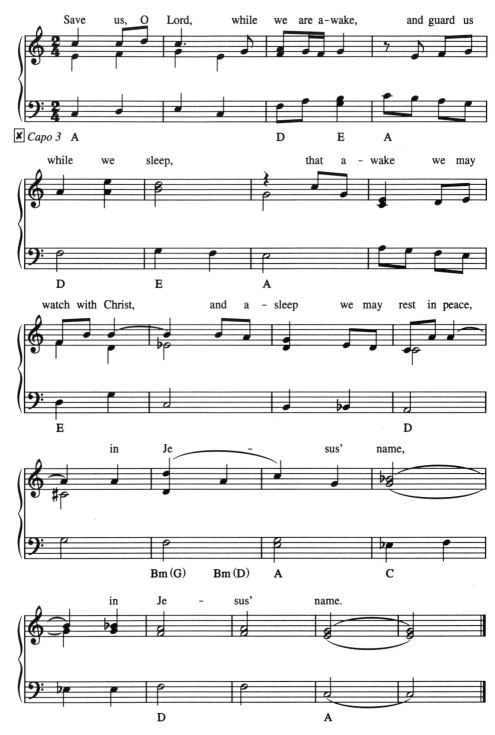

Words: Kevin Mayhew, based on the Office of Compline
Music: Kevin Mayhew, arr. Noel Rawsthorne

184 Seek ye first the kingdom of God

This may be sung as a round with the second voices entering at the refrain

2. You shall not live by bread alone,
   but by ev'ry word
   that proceeds from the mouth of God;
   allelu, alleluia.

3. Ask and it shall be given unto you,
   seek and ye shall find;
   knock and it shall be opened unto you;
   allelu, alleluia.

Words: verse 1: Karen Lafferty; verses 2 & 3: unknown, based on Matthew 6:33; 7:7
Music: Karen Lafferty, arr. Christopher Tambling

185 Set my heart on fire

giver of all good gifts,
so that keeping your commandments I may

glorify you, the giver of all good gifts.

Words: Kontakion (Eastern Orthodox Liturgy)
Music: Kevin Mayhew, arr. Noel Rawsthorne

186 Shalom, my friend

Shalom, my friend, shalom, my friend, sha-

lom, shalom. The peace of Christ I

give you today, shalom, shalom.

Words: Sandra Joan Billington
Music: traditional Hebrew melody, arr. Noel Rawsthorne

187 Sing glory to God
The Ash Grove Gloria

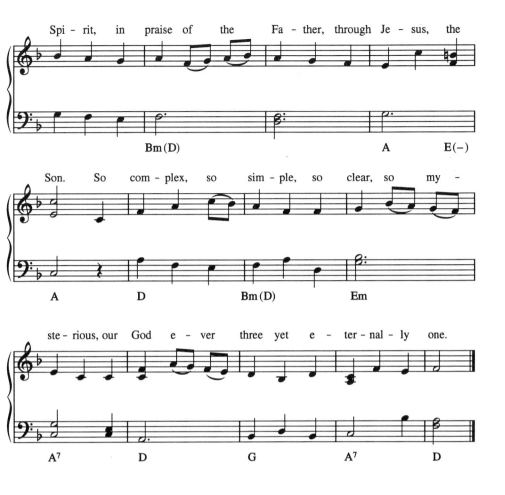

2. Lord Jesus, the Christ, only Son of the Father,
   the Lamb who has carried our burden of shame,
   now seated on high in the glory of heaven,
   have mercy upon us who call on your name.

3. For you, only you, we acknowledge as holy,
   we name you alone as our Saviour and Lord;
   you only, O Christ, with the Spirit exalted,
   at one with the Father, for ever adored.

Words: Michael Forster
Music: traditional Welsh melody, arr. Noel Rawsthorne

188 Sing praise to God

With a swing

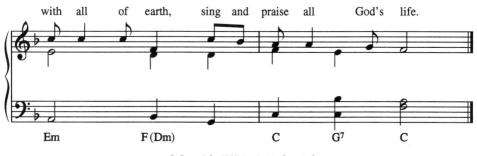

2. Lift up your eyes to see the works of God,
   in ev'ry blade of grass, in ev'ry human face.
   Lift up your eyes to see the works of God,
   through all of life, in all time and all space.

3. Open your ears to hear the cries of pain
   arising from the poor and all who are oppressed.
   Open your mind and use your wits to find
   who are the cause of this world's unjust ways.

4. Reach out your hands to share the wealth God gave
   with those who are oppressed, and those who feel alone.
   Reach out your hands and gently touch with Christ
   each frozen heart which has said 'No' to love.

5. Open our hearts to love the world with Christ,
   each person in this world, each creature of this earth.
   Open our hearts to love the ones who hate,
   and in their hearts find a part of ourself.

6. Live life with love, for love encircles all;
   it casts out all our fears, it fills the heart with joy.
   Live life with love, for love transforms our life,
   as we praise God with our eyes, hands and hearts.

Words: W.L. Wallace
Music: Noel Rawsthorne

189 Stand on the corner of the street
God is living everywhere

Cheerfully
Refrain

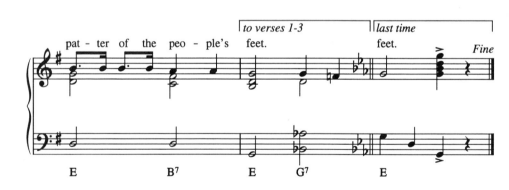

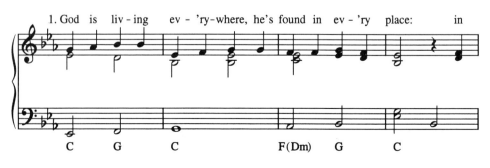

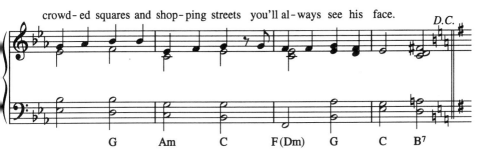

crowd-ed squares and shop-ping streets you'll al-ways see his face.

G   Am   C   F(Dm)   G   C   B⁷

2. God is living ev'rywhere
   that human life is found.
   In cafés, shops and car parks, too,
   his Spirit is around.

3. God is living ev'rywhere,
   in all the human race,
   in schools and flats and offices,
   in ev'rybody's face.

Words: Richard Farrow
Music: Andrew Gant

190 Stand up! Walk tall

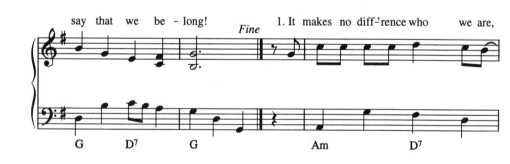

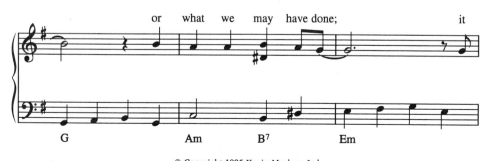

does – n't mat – ter where we're from, for

Am   D⁷   G

God loves ev – 'ry – one. Stand *D.S.*

A⁷   D   D⁷ (D)

2. Whatever people think or say,
   we need not be afraid.
   We're members of the human race,
   the people God has made.

3. So, male or female, black or white,
   of any age or race,
   we're not afraid to stand up straight
   and look God in the face!

Words: Michael Forster
Music: Christopher Tambling

191 Step by step, on and on
Jesus is the living way

Refrain

Step by step, on and on, we will walk with Je - sus till the

jour-ney's done. Step by step, day by day, be-cause

Je - sus is the liv- ing way. *Fine* 1. He's the one to

fol- low, in his foot- steps we will tread. Don't wor-ry a-bout to -

mor - row,   Je - sus knows the way   a - head.   Oh,

Em   A⁷   D

2. He will never leave us,
    and his love he'll always show,
    so wherever Jesus leads us,
    that's the way we want to go. Oh,

Words: Gill Hutchinson
Music: Gill Hutchinson, arr. Noel Rawsthorne

192 Thank you for the summer morning

1. Thank you for the sum-mer morn-ing, mist-ing in - to heat;

Capo 5   C   Am   Dm   G⁷

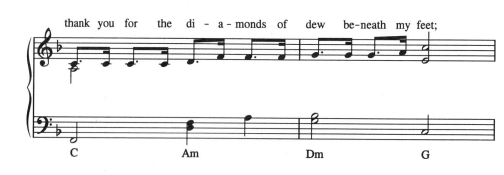

thank you for the di - a - monds of dew be-neath my feet;

C   Am   Dm   G

thank you for the sil - ver where a snail has wan-dered by; oh, we

F (Dm)   Am   Dm   G

to verses 1 - 3
praise the name of him who made the earth and sea and sky.

last time
earth and sea and sky.

D.C.

C   F (Dm)   Dm   G⁷   Dm   G⁷   C

2. Thank you for the yellow fields
   of corn like waving hair;
   thank you for the red surprise
   of poppies here and there;
   thank you for the blue of
   an electric dragonfly;
   oh, we praise the name
   of him who made
   the earth and sea and sky.

3. Thank you for the splintered light
   among the brooding trees;
   thank you for the leaves that rustle
   in a sudden breeze;
   thank you for the branches
   and the fun of climbing high;
   oh, we praise the name
   of him who made
   the earth and sea and sky.

4. Thank you for the ev'ning
   as the light begins to fade;
   clouds so red and purple
   that the setting sun has made;
   thank you for the shadows
   as the owls come gliding by;
   oh, we praise the name
   of him who made
   the earth and sea and sky.

Words: Susan Sayers
Music: Susan Sayers, arr. Noel Rawsthorne

193 Thank you, Lord
Right where you are

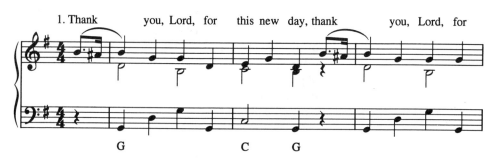

1. Thank you, Lord, for this new day, thank you, Lord, for

G   C   G

this new day, thank you, Lord, for this new day,

D⁷   G   C   G

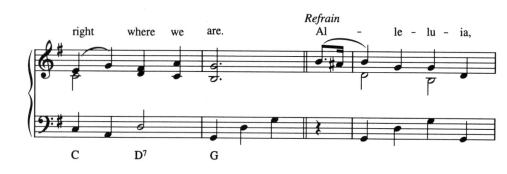

right where we are.   *Refrain*   Al - le - lu - ia,

C   D⁷   G

praise the Lord, al - le - lu - ia, praise the Lord, al -

C   G   D⁷

le - lu - ia, praise the Lord, right where we are.

G C G C D⁷ G

2. Thank you, Lord, for food to eat,
   thank you, Lord, for food to eat,
   thank you, Lord, for food to eat,
   right where we are.

3. Thank you, Lord, for clothes to wear,
   thank you, Lord, for clothes to wear,
   thank you, Lord, for clothes to wear,
   right where we are.

4. Thank you, Lord, for all your gifts,
   thank you, Lord, for all your gifts,
   thank you, Lord, for all your gifts,
   right where we are.

Words: Diane Davis Andrew, adapted by Geoffrey Marshall-Taylor
Music: Diane Davis Andrew, arr. Noel Rawsthorne

194 The bell of creation

In waltz time

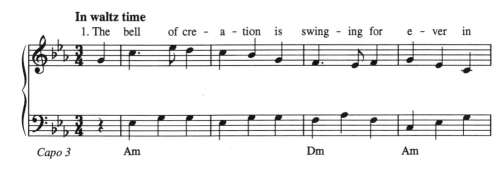

1. The bell of cre - a - tion is swing - ing for e - ver in

Capo 3   Am   Dm   Am

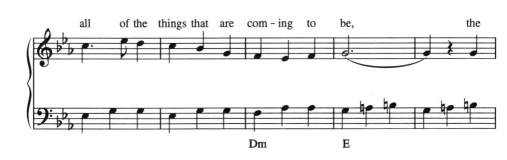

all of the things that are com - ing to be,   the

Dm   E

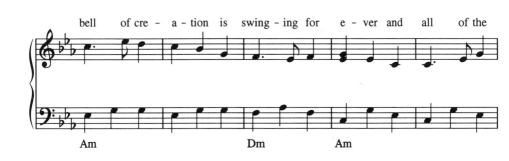

bell of cre - a - tion is swing - ing for e - ver and all of the

Am   Dm   Am

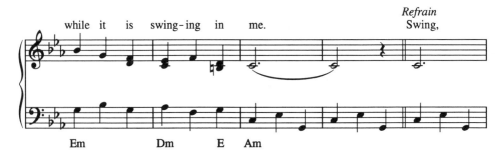

while it is swing-ing in me.   *Refrain* Swing,

Em   Dm   E   Am

2. In all of my loving, in all of my labour,
   in all of the things that are coming to be,
   in all of my loving, in all of my labour,
   the bell of creation is swinging in me.

3. I look to the life that is living for ever
   in all of the things that are coming to be,
   I look to the life that is living for ever,
   and all of the while it is looking for me.

4. I'll swing with the bell that is swinging for ever,
   in all of the things that are coming to be,
   I'll swing with the bell that is swinging for ever,
   and all of the while it is swinging in me.

Words: Sydney Carter
Music: Sydney Carter, arr. Noel Rawsthorne

195 The clock tells the story of time

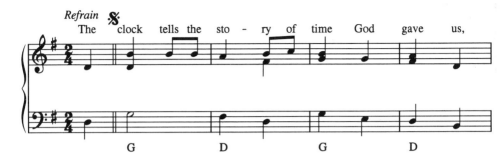

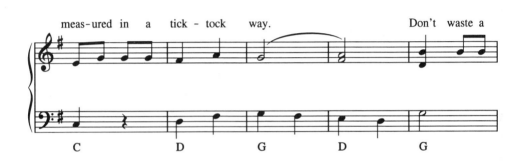

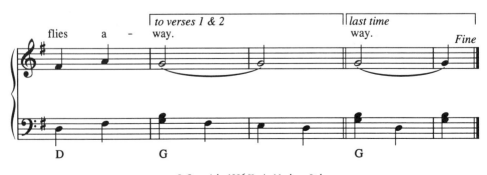

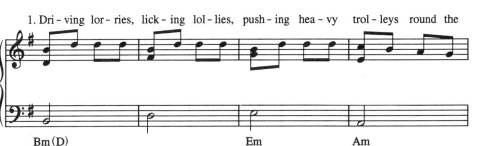

1. Dri - ving lor - ries, lick - ing lol - lies, push - ing hea - vy trol - leys round the

Bm (D)   Em   Am

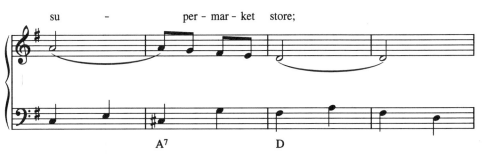

su - per - mar - ket store;

A⁷   D

wash - ing fa - ces, ty - ing la - ces, blink - ing, wink - ing, drink - ing and much

Am   D   Bm (D)

more you can be sure. The
D.S.

Em   A   G   D

2. Time is good for thinking in,
   for helping other people in,
   or playing with a friend;
   time is like a funny kind of
   pocket money given
   ev'ry day for us to spend.

Words: Susan Sayers
Music: Susan Sayers, arr. Noel Rawsthorne

196 The duck goes 'Quack'

2. The cow goes 'Moo',
   the cow goes 'Moo'.
   She gives good milk to me and you.
   The cow goes 'Moo',
   the cow goes 'Moo'.
   I'm glad that God made cows.

3. The horse goes 'Neigh',
   the horse goes 'Neigh'.
   It likes to run and eat good hay.
   The horse goes 'Neigh',
   the horse goes 'Neigh'.
   I'm glad God made the horse.

4. The cat goes 'Purr',
   the cat goes 'Purr'.
   I like to pet her soft warm fur.
   The cat goes 'Purr',
   the cat goes 'Purr'.
   I'm glad that God made cats.

5. The dog can bark,
   the dog can bark.
   It likes to run around the park.
   The dog can bark,
   the dog can bark.
   I'm glad that God made dogs.

Words: B.C. Hanson
Music: B.C. Hanson, arr. Norman Warren

197 The King is among us

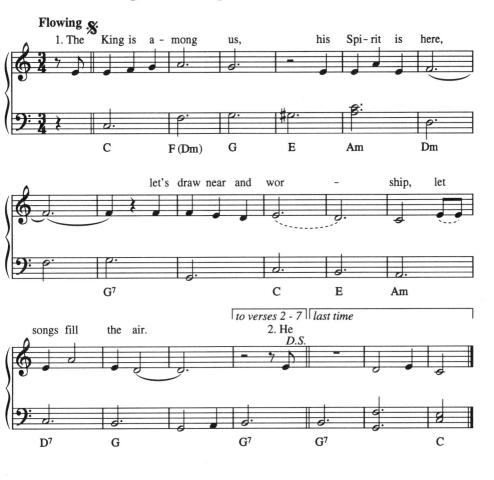

Flowing 𝄋

1. The King is a-mong us, his Spi-rit is here,
let's draw near and wor - ship, let
songs fill the air.

to verses 2 - 7 | *last time*
2. He
D.S.

Chords: C F (Dm) G E Am Dm G7 C E Am D7 G G7 G7 C

2. He looks down upon us,
   delight in his face,
   enjoying his children's love,
   enthralled by our praise.

3. For each child is special,
   accepted and loved,
   a love-gift from Jesus
   to his Father above.

4. And now he is giving
   his gifts to us all,
   for no one is worthless
   and each one is called.

5. The Spirit's anointing
   on all flesh comes down,
   and we shall be channels
   for works like his own.

6. We come now believing
   your promise of pow'r,
   for we are your people
   and this is your hour.

7. The King is among us,
   his Spirit is here,
   let's draw near and worship,
   let songs fill the air.

Words: Graham Kendrick
Music: Graham Kendrick, arr. Christopher Tambling

198 The Spirit lives to set us free
Walk in the light

1. The Spi-rit lives to set us free, walk, walk in the light. He

G Bm(D) C G C D G C(-) G

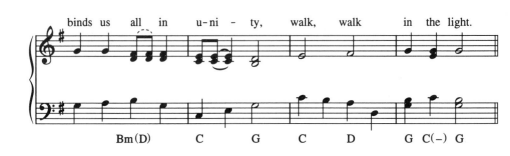

binds us all in u-ni-ty, walk, walk in the light.

Bm(D) C G C D G C(-) G

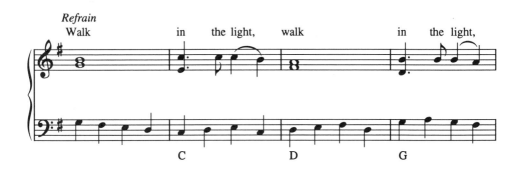

Refrain

Walk in the light, walk in the light,

C D G

walk in the light, walk in the light of the Lord. Lord.

to verses 3-6 | to verse 2 & last time

Em Am D⁷ G G

2. Jesus promised life to all,
   walk, walk in the light.
   The dead were wakened by his call,
   walk, walk in the light.

3. He died in pain on Calvary,
   walk, walk in the light,
   to save the lost like you and me,
   walk, walk in the light.

4. We know his death was not the end,
   walk, walk in the light.
   He gave his Spirit to be our friend,
   walk, walk in the light.

5. By Jesus' love our wounds are healed,
   walk, walk in the light.
   The Father's kindness is revealed,
   walk, walk in the light.

6. The Spirit lives in you and me,
   walk, walk in the light.
   His light will shine for all to see,
   walk, walk in the light.

Words: Damian Lundy
Music: unknown, arr. Noel Rawsthorne

199 The voice from the bush
Lead my people to freedom

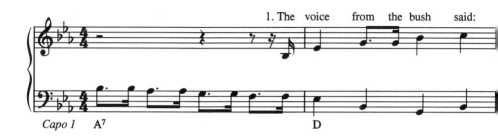

1. The voice from the bush said:

Capo 1 A⁷   D

Mo-ses, look snap-py, have I got a job for you!

D⁷ (D)   G   A⁷   D

I've looked a-round and I'm not ve-ry hap-py. Here is what you have to

E   E⁷ (E)   A

do:
Refrain
Lead my peo - ple to free - dom!

A⁷ (A)   D   D⁷ (D)

2. The people of God were suff'ring and dying,
   sick and tired of slavery.
   All God could hear was the sound of their crying;
   Moses had to set them free.

3. We know that the world is still full of sorrow,
   people need to be set free.
   We've got to give them a better tomorrow,
   so God says to you and me:

Words: Michael Forster
Music: Christopher Tambling

200 The wise man built his house upon the rock

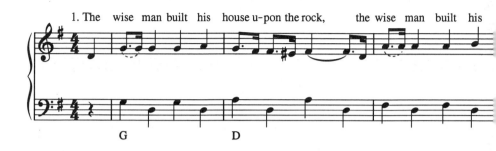

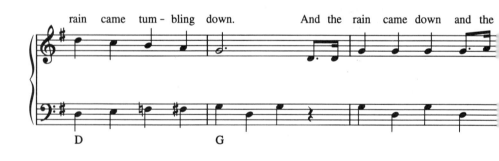

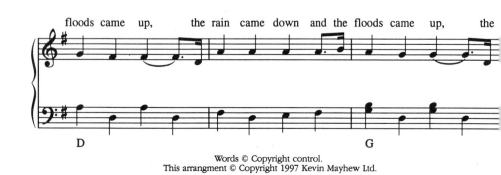

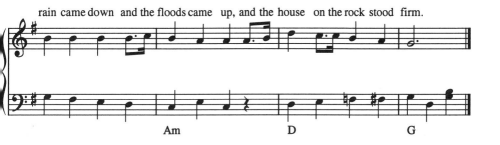

rain came down and the floods came up, and the house on the rock stood firm.

Am   D   G

2. The foolish man built his house upon the sand,
   the foolish man built his house upon the sand,
   the foolish man built his house upon the sand,
   and the rain came tumbling down.
   And the rain came down and the floods came up,
   the rain came down and the floods came up,
   the rain came down and the floods came up,
   and the house on the sand fell flat.

Words: unknown
Music: unknown, arr. Noel Rawsthorne

201 The world is full of smelly feet

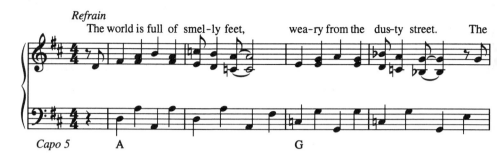

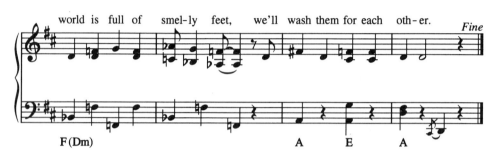

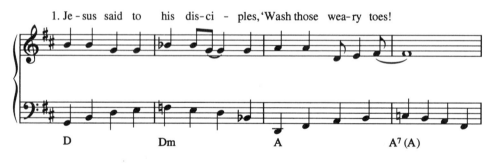

2. People on a dusty journey
   need a place to rest;
   Jesus says, 'You say you love me,
   this will be the test!'

3. We're his friends, we recognise him
   in the folk we meet;
   smart or scruffy, we'll still love him,
   wash his smelly feet!

Words: Michael Forster
Music: Christopher Tambling

© Copyright 1997 Kevin Mayhew Ltd.

202 There are hundreds of sparrows
God knows me

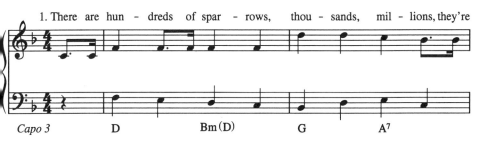

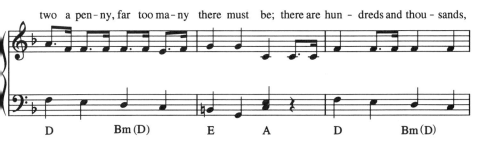

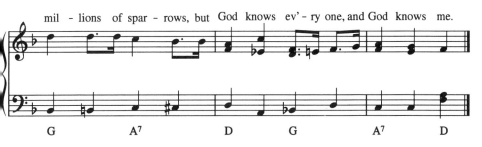

2. There are hundreds of flowers, thousands, millions,
   and flowers fair the meadows wear for all to see;
   there are hundreds and thousands, millions of flowers,
   but God knows ev'ry one, and God knows me.

3. There are hundreds of planets, thousands, millions,
   way out in space each has a place by God's decree;
   there are hundreds and thousands, millions of planets,
   but God knows ev'ry one, and God knows me.

4. There are hundreds of children, thousands, millions,
   and yet their names are written on God's memory;
   there are hundreds and thousands, millions of children,
   but God knows ev'ry one, and God knows me.

Words: John Gowans
Music: John Larsson, arr. Noel Rawsthorne

203 There are people who live in mansions
Gotta put the world to rights

2. There are people who feed on salmon,
   there are people who feed on stew,
   there are people who hardly feed at all,
   and God says that won't do!

3. There are people with famous faces,
   there are people with famous names,
   there are people whom no one knows at a[ll,]
   and God says that's a shame.

Words: Dave Davidson
Music: Noel Rawsthorne

204 There is a green hill

1. There is a green hill far a - way, out - side a ci - ty wall, where

Capo 2   C   Dm⁷   G⁷   C   D⁷   G

Christ our Lord was cru - ci - fied, who died to save us all.

G⁷   C   F   E   F   G⁷   C

2. We may not know, we cannot tell,
   what pains he had to bear,
   but we believe it was for us
   he hung and suffered there.

3. He died that we could be forgiv'n,
   that God might call us good,
   that we might go at last to heav'n,
   saved by his precious blood.

4. O dearly, dearly has he loved,
   so let us love him too,
   and trust in his redeeming blood,
   and try his works to do.

Words: Cecil Frances Alexander, alt.
Music: William Horsley, arr. Noel Rawsthorne

205 There was one, there were two
The children's band

Lightly

Refrain

There was one, there were two, there were three friends of Je-sus, there were four, there were five, there were six friends of Je-sus, there were sev'n, there were eight, there were nine friends of Je-sus, ten friends of Je-sus in the band.

Fine

1. Bells are going to ring in praise of Je-sus, praise of Je-sus, praise of

Je - sus, bells are going to ring in praise of

Je - sus, prais - ing Je - sus the Lord.

D.C.

D⁷   G

. Drums are going to boom in praise of Jesus,
praise of Jesus, praise of Jesus,
drums are going to boom in praise of Jesus,
praising Jesus the Lord.

. Tambourines will shake in praise of Jesus,
praise of Jesus, praise of Jesus,
tambourines will shake in praise of Jesus,
praising Jesus the Lord.

. Trumpets will resound in praise of Jesus,
praise of Jesus, praise of Jesus,
trumpets will resound in praise of Jesus,
praising Jesus the Lord.

Verses may be added ad lib, for example:

Clarinets will swing in praise of Jesus . . .

Play recorders, too . . .

Triangles will ting . . .

Fiddles will be scraped . . .

Let guitars be strummed . . .

Chime bars will be chimed . . .

Glockenspiels will play . . .

Vibraphones will throb . . .

Trombones slide about . . .

Words: Christina Wilde
Music: traditional American melody, arr. Noel Rawsthorne

206 There's a great big world out there

2. We've brought to God our prayers and hymns,
   now it's time to live his life,
   to sow a little love and peace
   in the place of selfish strife.

3. We've listened to the word of God,
   now it's time to live it out,
   to show by ev'rything we do
   what the gospel is about.

This may be sung as a round during the third verse with the second voices entering at the refrain (using the accompaniment to the verse).

Words: Michael Forster
Music: Andrew Gant

207 There's a rainbow in the sky

Refrain

There's a rain-bow in the sky, and it's o-kay! There's a

G E Am Cdim⁷(–)

rain-bow in the sky, and it's o-kay! There's a rain-bow in the sky, and it's o-

D⁷ G B⁷ Em G⁷

kay! It's a sign that God is good. *Fine*

Am A⁷ D⁷ G

1. For-ty days and nights a-float, all cooped up on No-ah's boat!

C G D⁷ G Am G Am D

Now the rain is al-most done; wake up world, here comes the sun!

C   G   D⁷   G   D   Bm (D)   Em   A⁷   D

2. Now we've got another start,
   ev'ryone can play a part:
   make the world a better place,
   put a smile on ev'ry face!

3. Sometimes, still, the world is bad,
   people hungry, people sad.
   Jesus wants us all to care,
   showing people ev'rywhere:

Words: Michael Forster
Music: Christopher Tambling

208 There's a seed

1. There's a seed in a flow'r on a plant in a gar-den of the world, as it
swirls through the wide-ness of space... of our star-speck-led ga-la-xy,
speck of the u-ni-verse, made and sus-tained by the love of our God.

Refrain

Capo 1   A   E   A   E   A
F#m (A)   A   B⁷   E   A   E
A   E   A   D   A   E   A

2. There's an ant in a nest
   on the floor of a forest
   of the world, as it swirls
   through the wideness of space . . .

3. There's a crab in a shell,
   in the depth of an ocean
   of the world, as it swirls
   through the wideness of space . . .

4. There's a child in a school
   of a town in a country
   of the world, as it swirls
   through the wideness of space . . .

Words: Susan Sayers
Music: Susan Sayers, arr. Noel Rawsthorne

209 Think big: an elephant

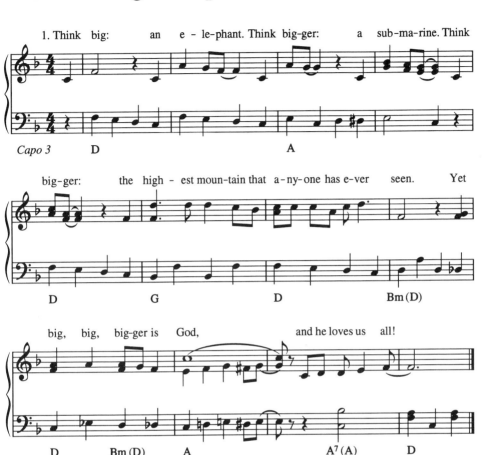

Capo 3

2. Think old: a vintage car.
   Think older: a full grown tree.
   Think older: a million grains
   of the sand beside the surging sea.
   Yet old, old, older is God,
   and he loves us all!

3. Think strong: a tiger's jaw.
   Think stronger: a castle wall.
   Think stronger: a hurricane
   that leaves little standing there at all.
   Yet strong, strong, stronger is God,
   and he loves us all!

Words: Susan Sayers
Music: Susan Sayers, arr. Noel Rawsthorne

210 Think of a world without any flowers

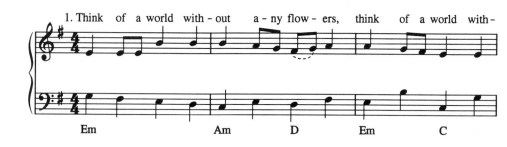

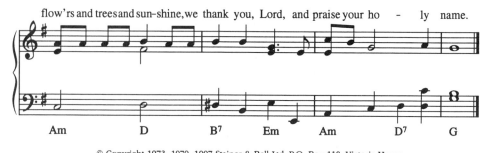

2. Think of a world without any animals,
   think of a field without any herd,
   think of a stream without any fishes,
   think of a dawn without any bird.
   We thank you, Lord, for all your living creatures,
   we thank you, Lord, and praise your holy name.

3. Think of a world without any people,
   think of a street with no one living there,
   think of a town without any houses,
   no one to love and nobody to care.
   We thank you, Lord, for families and friendships,
   we thank you, Lord, and praise your holy name.

Words: Doreen Newport
Music: Graham Westcott, arr. Noel Rawsthorne

211 This is the day

Brightly, with pace

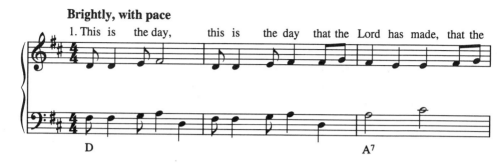

1. This is the day, this is the day that the Lord has made, that the

D   A⁷

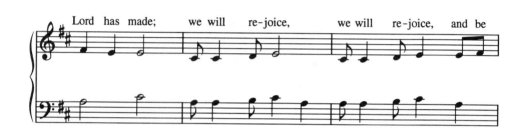

Lord has made; we will re-joice, we will re-joice, and be

glad in it, and be glad in it. This is the day that the

D   D⁷ (D)   G

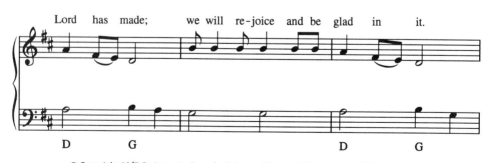

Lord has made; we will re-joice and be glad in it.

D   G   D   G

This is the day, this is the day that the Lord has made.

D   A⁷   D

2. This is the day, this is the day
   when he rose again, when he rose again;
   we will rejoice, we will rejoice,
   and be glad in it, and be glad in it.
   This is the day when he rose again;
   we will rejoice and be glad in it.
   This is the day, this is the day
   when he rose again.

3. This is the day, this is the day
   when the Spirit came, when the Spirit came;
   we will rejoice, we will rejoice,
   and be glad in it, and be glad in it.
   This is the day when the Spirit came;
   we will rejoice and be glad in it.
   This is the day, this is the day
   when the Spirit came.

Words: Les Garrett
Music: Les Garrett, arr. Noel Rawsthorne

212 This little light of mine

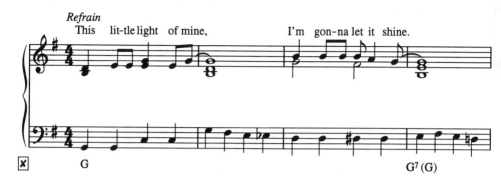

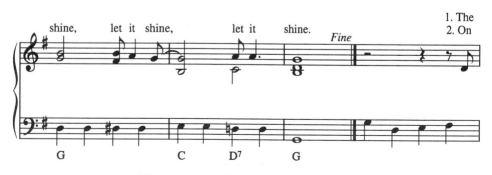

Words: traditional, alt.
Music: traditional, arr. Noel Rawsthorne

213 This world you have made
Beautiful world

Refrain

This world you have made is a beau-ti-ful place, it tells the pow'r of your

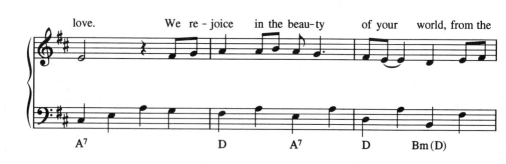

love. We re - joice in the beau-ty of your world, from the

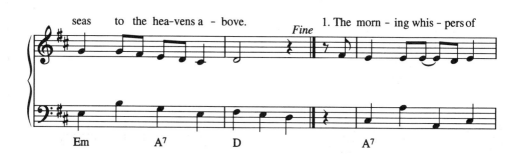

seas to the hea-vens a - bove. *Fine* 1. The morn - ing whis - pers of

pu - ri - ty; the gath-er-ing dark - ness, peace; the

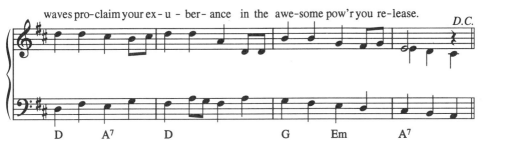

waves pro-claim your ex- u – ber- ance in the awe-some pow'r you re-lease.

D.C.

D   A⁷   D   G   Em   A⁷

2. The tenderness of a new-born child,
   the gentleness of the rain,
   simplicity in a single cell,
   and complexity in a brain.

3. Your stillness rests in a silent pool,
   infinity drifts in space;
   your grandeur straddles the mountain tops,
   and we see your face in each face.

Words: Susan Sayers
Music: Susan Sayers, arr. Noel Rawsthorne

214 Tick tock

This may be sung as a round, with voices at A *,* B *,* C *and* D

Words: Alan J. Price
Music: Alan J. Price, arr. Noel Rawsthorne

215 Wait for the Lord

Refrain
Wait for the Lord, whose day is near.

Wait for the Lord: keep watch, take heart! *Fine*

Pre - pare the way for the Lord. Make a straight path for him. *D.C.*

Words: from Scripture
Music: Jacques Berthier

The
Children's
Hymn
Book

216 Waiting for your Spirit

Words: Mick Gisbey
Music: Mick Gisbey, arr. Noel Rawsthorne

217 Walk with me, O my Lord

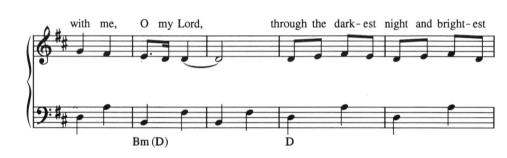

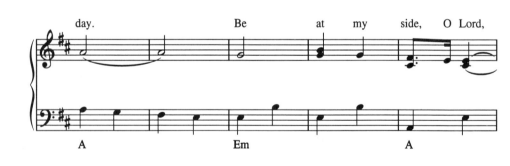

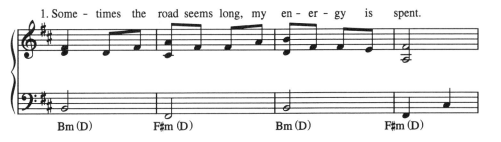

1. Some - times the road seems long, my en - er - gy is spent.

Bm (D)　　　F♯m (D)　　　Bm (D)　　　F♯m (D)

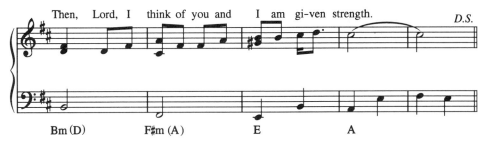

Then, Lord, I think of you and I am gi-ven strength.　　*D.S.*

Bm (D)　　　F♯m (A)　　　E　　　A

2. Stones often bar my path,
   and there are times I fall,
   but you are always there
   to help me when I call.

3. Just as you calmed the wind
   and walked upon the sea,
   conquer, my living Lord,
   the storms that threaten me.

4. Help me to pierce the mists
   that cloud my heart and mind,
   so that I shall not fear
   the steepest mountainside.

5. As once you healed the lame
   and gave sight to the blind,
   help me, when I'm downcast,
   to hold my head up high.

Words: Estelle White
Music: Estelle White, arr. Noel Rawsthorne

218 We are marching in the light of God

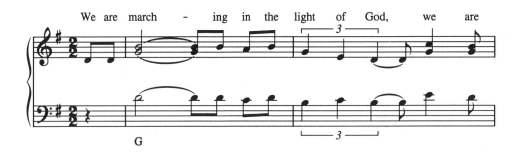

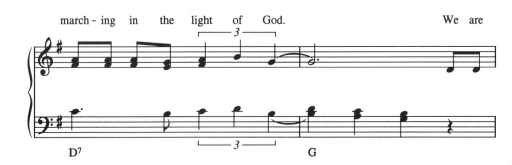

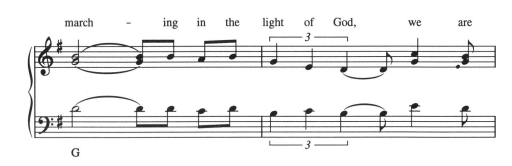

* Optional 2nd part

To create further verses, 'marching' may be replaced with 'dancing', 'singing', 'praying', etc.

Words: traditional South African, trans. Anders Nyberg
Music: traditional South African, arr. Noel Rawsthorne

The
Children's
Hymn
Book

219 We are one family together

Gently

1. We are one fa-mi-ly to-ge - ther, we are one fa-mi-ly in God. We are one fa-mi-ly to-ge - ther, the whole earth is our home.

2. We care for creatures and for plant life,
   we care for ev'rything that lives.
   We care for soil, for air and water,
   the whole earth is our home.

3. We care for children and for adults,
   we care for those who are oppressed.
   We care for justice and for sharing,
   the whole earth is our home.

4. We are one family together,
   we are one family in God.
   We are one family together,
   the whole earth is our home.

Words: W.L. Wallace
Music: Norman Warren

220 We can plough and dig the land

Joyfully

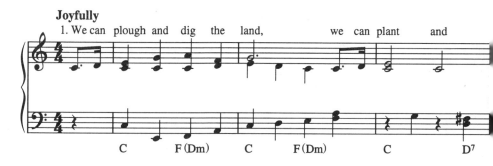

1. We can plough and dig the land, we can plant and

sow, we can wa - ter, we can weed, but we

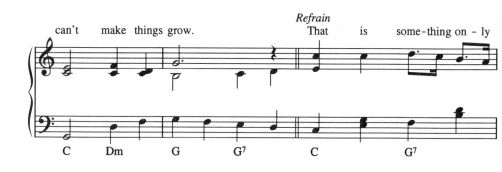

can't make things grow. *Refrain* That is some-thing on - ly

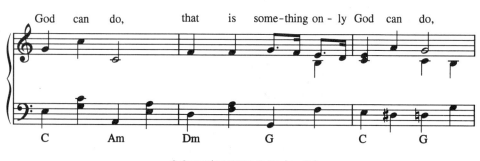

God can do, that is some-thing on - ly God can do,

that is some-thing on-ly God can do, on-ly God can make things grow.

2. We can edge and we can prune,
   we can rake and hoe,
   we can lift and we can feed,
   but we can't make things grow.

3. We can watch the little shoots
   sprouting row by row,
   we can hope and we can pray,
   but we can't make things grow.

Words: Michael Forster
Music: Christopher Tambling

221 We eat the plants that grow from the seed

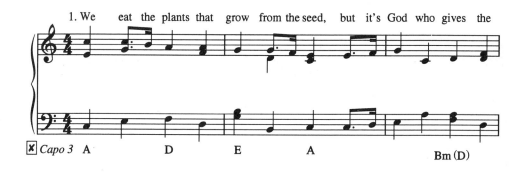

1. We eat the plants that grow from the seed, but it's God who gives the

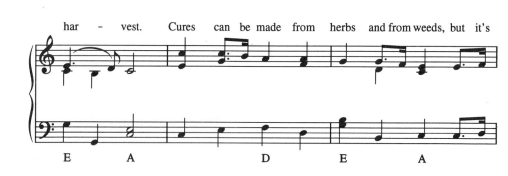

har - vest. Cures can be made from herbs and from weeds, but it's

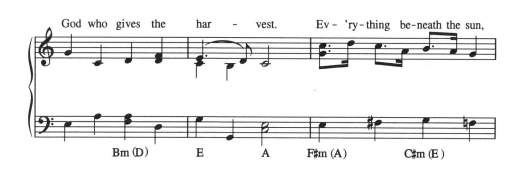

God who gives the har - vest. Ev - 'ry-thing be-neath the sun,

all the things we claim we've done, all are part of God's cre -

2. We find the iron and turn it to steel,
   but it's God who gives the harvest.
   We pull the levers, we turn the wheels,
   but it's God who gives the harvest.
   Ev'rything we say we've made,
   plastic bags to metal spades,
   all are part of God's creation:
   we can make lots of things
   from microchips to springs,
   but it's God who gives the harvest.

Words: Susan Mee
Music: traditional English melody, arr. Noel Rawsthorne

222 We have a King who rides a donkey

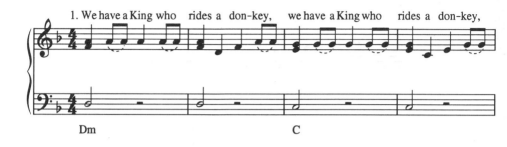

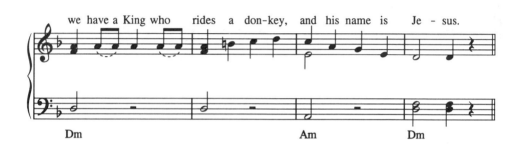

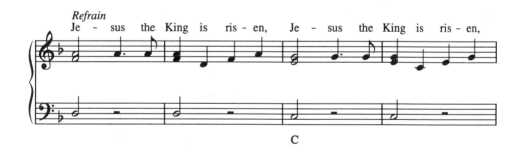

2. Trees are waving a royal welcome,
    trees are waving a royal welcome,
    trees are waving a royal welcome
    for the King called Jesus.

3. We have a King who cares for people,
    we have a King who cares for people,
    we have a King who cares for people
    and his name is Jesus.

4. A loaf and a cup upon the table,
    a loaf and a cup upon the table,
    a loaf and a cup upon the table,
    bread-and-wine is Jesus.

5. We have a King with a bowl and towel,
    we have a King with a bowl and towel,
    we have a King with a bowl and towel,
    Servant-King is Jesus.

6. What shall we do with our life this morning?
    What shall we do with our life this morning?
    What shall we do with our life this morning?
    Give it up in service!

Verse 4 is suitable for Communion.

Words: Fred Kaan
Music: traditional, arr. Noel Rawsthorne

223 We plough the fields, and scatter

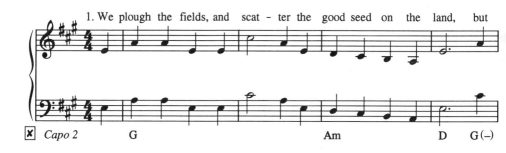

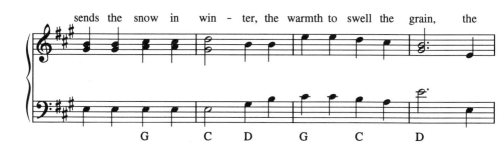

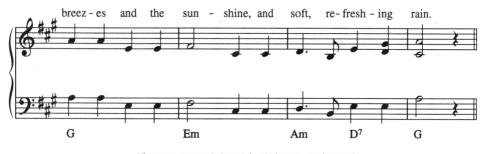

Words: Matthias Claudius, trans. Jane Montgomery Campbell, alt.
Music: Johann Schulz, arr. Alan Ridout

Refrain

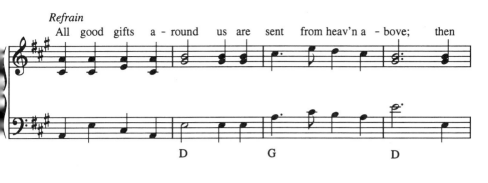

All good gifts a - round us are sent from heav'n a - bove; then

D   G   D

thank the Lord, O thank the Lord, for all his love.

G   Em   Am   D⁷   G

2. He only is the maker
   of all things near and far;
   he paints the wayside flower,
   he lights the evening star.
   He fills the earth with beauty,
   by him the birds are fed;
   much more to us, his children,
   he gives our daily bread.

3. We thank thee, then, O Father,
   for all things bright and good:
   the seed-time and the harvest,
   our life, our health, our food.
   Accept the gifts we offer
   for all thy love imparts,
   and, what thou most desirest,
   our humble, thankful hearts.

224 We thank God for the harvest
Gotta get out and scatter some seed

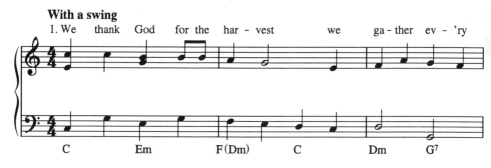

1. We thank God for the har-vest we ga-ther ev-'ry

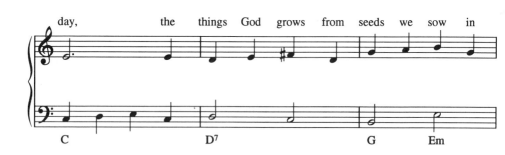

day, the things God grows from seeds we sow in

all our work and play. *Refrain* Got-ta get out and scat-ter some

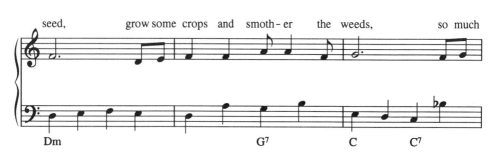

seed, grow some crops and smoth-er the weeds, so much

love there's no room for greed, got-ta go and scat-ter some seeds.

F (Dm)   G   C   G⁷   C

2. God gives love to be scattered,
   and seeds of faith to sow,
   then sprinkles grace in ev'ry place
   to make the harvest grow.

3. We can work all together,
   with people ev'rywhere:
   in ev'ry place, each creed and race,
   God gives us love to share.

Words: Christine Wilde
Music: Noel Rawsthorne

225 We will praise

Words: Ian Smale
Music: Ian Smale, arr. Noel Rawsthorne

226 We're going to shine like the sun
No one will ever be the same

Leader

1. We're going to shine like the sun in the king-dom of hea - ven,

G   Am   B⁷   Em

All

shine like the sun in the king-dom of heav'n; we're going to

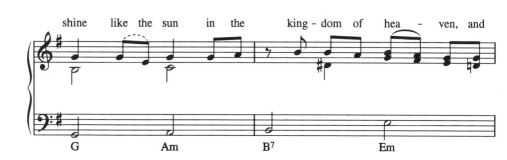

C   G   C   D⁷

shine like the sun in the king-dom of hea - ven, and

G   Am   B⁷   Em

no one will e-ver be the same.   *Refrain* And it's all in Je-sus'

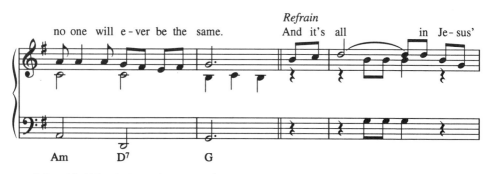

Am   D⁷   G

name;   and it's all   in Je - sus' name;   yes, it's

all   in Je- sus' name   that no one will e- ver be the same.

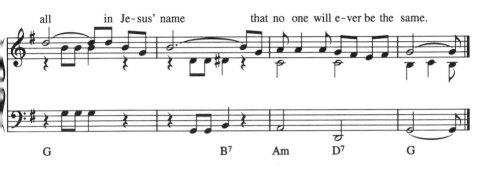

2. We're going to learn from the poor in the kingdom of heaven,
learn from the poor in the kingdom of heav'n;
we're going to learn from the poor in the kingdom of heaven,
and no one will ever be the same.

3. We're going to walk with the weak in the kingdom of heaven,
walk with the weak in the kingdom of heav'n;
we're going to walk with the weak in the kingdom of heaven,
and no one will ever be the same.

4. We're going to drink the new wine in the kingdom of heaven,
drink the new wine in the kingdom of heav'n;
we're going to drink the new wine in the kingdom of heaven,
and no one will ever be the same.

5. And it all starts now in the kingdom of heaven,
all starts now in the kingdom of heav'n;
and it all starts now in the kingdom of heaven,
and no one will ever be the same.

Words: John L. Bell and Graham Maule
Music: John L. Bell and Graham Maule, arr. Norman Warren

The
Children's
Hymn
Book

227 What kind of man was this

Freely

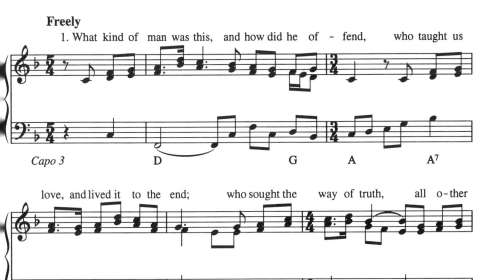

2. What kind of man was this, so full of truth divine,
   who turned the foulest water into wine;
   who called us to his side, and gave us all a place?
   What kind of man was this, what kind of grace?

3. What kind of man was this, who opened up his heart
   to those who sought to tear his flesh apart;
   whose all-forgiving words his perfect nature prove?
   What kind of man was this, what kind of love?

4. What kind of man was this, who helped us all to see
   the fullness of our human dignity?
   So hopeful in despair, so noble in disgrace,
   what kind of man was this, what kind of grace?

Words: Michael Forster
Music: Christopher Tambling

228 When God made the garden of creation

Brightly

1. When God made the gar-den of cre-a - tion, he filled it full of his love;

Capo 2   C   F(Dm)   C   G⁷   C

when God made the gar-den of cre-a - tion, he saw that it was

F(Dm)   C   G⁷

good.   There's room for you, and room for me, and room for ev - 'ry-

C   F(Dm)   B⁷   Em   A   Dm   G⁷

one: for God   is a Fa - ther who loves his child - ren, and

C   F(Dm)   B⁷   Em   A

gives them a place   in the sun.   When God made   the

D   G⁷   C

© Copyright Mr. Paul Booth. Used by permission.

gar - den of cre - a - tion, he filled it full of his love.

F (Dm)   C   G⁷   C

2. When God made the hamper of creation,
   he filled it full of his love;
   when God made the hamper of creation,
   he saw that it was good.
   There's food for you, and food for me,
   and food for ev'ryone:
   but often we're greedy, and waste God's bounty,
   so some don't get any at all.
   When God made the hamper of creation,
   he filled it full of his love.

3. When God made the fam'ly of creation,
   he made it out of his love;
   when God made the fam'ly of creation,
   he saw that it was good.
   There's love for you, and love for me,
   and love for ev'ryone:
   but sometimes we're selfish, ignore our neighbours,
   and seek our own place in the sun.
   When God made the fam'ly of creation,
   he made it out of his love.

4. When God made the garden of creation,
   he filled it full of his love;
   when God made the garden of creation,
   he saw that it was good.
   There's room for you, and room for me,
   and room for ev'ryone:
   for God is a Father who loves his children,
   and gives them a place in the sun.
   When God made the garden of creation,
   he filled it full of his love.

Words: Paul Booth
Music: Paul Booth, arr. Norman Warren

229 When I needed a neighbour

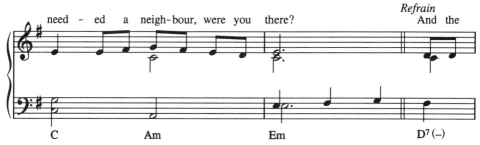

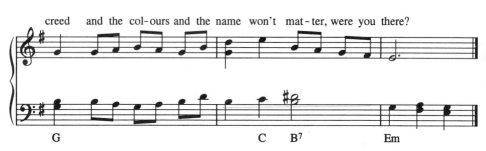

2. I was hungry and thirsty,
   were you there, were you there?
   I was hungry and thirsty,
   were you there?

3. I was cold, I was naked,
   were you there, were you there?
   I was cold, I was naked,
   were you there?

4. When I needed a shelter
   were you there, were you there?
   When I needed a shelter
   were you there?

5. When I needed a healer
   were you there, were you there?
   When I needed a healer
   were you there?

6. Wherever you travel
   I'll be there, I'll be there,
   wherever you travel
   I'll be there.

Last refrain:
And the creed and the colour
and the name won't matter,
I'll be there.

Words: Sydney Carter
Music: Sydney Carter, arr. Noel Rawsthorne

230 When Jesus was my age

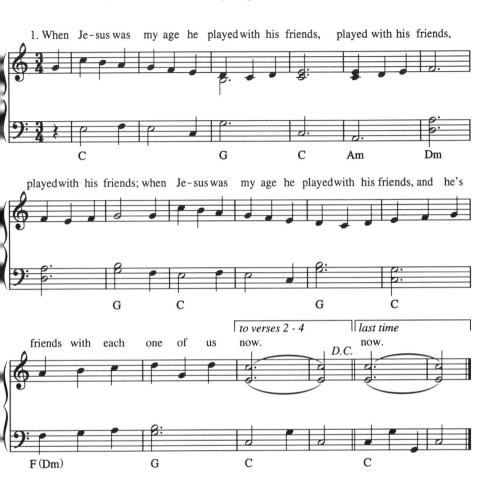

2. When Jesus was my age he laughed and he sang,
laughed and he sang, laughed and he sang;
when Jesus was my age he laughed and he sang,
and he loves hearing us singing now.

3. When Jesus was my age he sometimes felt sad,
sometimes felt sad, sometimes felt sad;
when Jesus was my age he sometimes felt sad,
and he shares in our sadnesses now.

4. When Jesus was my age he went to his school,
went to his school, went to his school;
when Jesus was my age he went to his school,
and he goes ev'rywhere with us now.

231 When the Spirit of the Lord

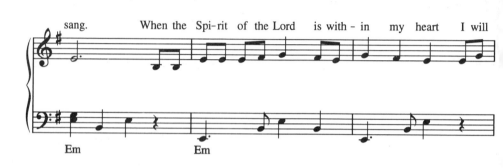

This arrangement © Copyright 1997 Kevin Mayhew Ltd.

sing,   I will sing,   I will sing as Da - vid sang.

Am   Em   B⁷   Em

2. When the Spirit of the Lord is within my heart
    I will clap as David clapped.
    When the Spirit of the Lord is within my heart
    I will clap as David clapped.
    I will clap, I will clap,
    I will clap as David clapped.
    I will clap, I will clap,
    I will clap as David clapped.

3. When the Spirit of the Lord is within my heart
    I will dance as David danced.
    When the Spirit of the Lord is within my heart
    I will dance as David danced.
    I will dance, I will dance,
    I will dance as David danced.
    I will dance, I will dance,
    I will dance as David danced.

4. When the Spirit of the Lord is within my heart
    I will praise as David praised.
    When the Spirit of the Lord is within my heart
    I will praise as David praised.
    I will praise, I will praise,
    I will praise as David praised.
    I will praise, I will praise,
    I will praise as David praised.

Words: unknown
Music: unknown, arr. Noel Rawsthorne

232 When your Father made the world
Care for your world

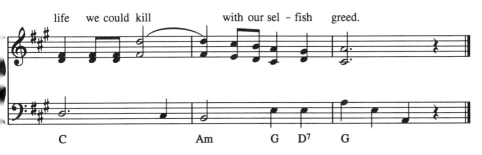

2. All the world that he had made,
   the seas, the rocks, the air,
   all the creatures and the plants he gave into our care.
   Help your people to care for your world.

3. When you walked in Galilee,
   you said your Father knows
   when each tiny sparrow dies, each fragile lily grows.
   Help your people to care for your world.

4. And the children of the earth,
   like sheep within your fold,
   should have food enough to eat, and shelter from the cold.
   Help your people to care for your world.

Words: Anne Conlon
Music: Peter Rose, arr. Norman Warren

233 Whether you're one

Joyfully

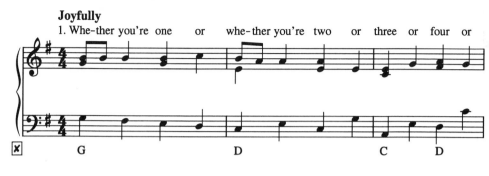

1. Whe-ther you're one or whe-ther you're two or three or four or

G   D   C   D

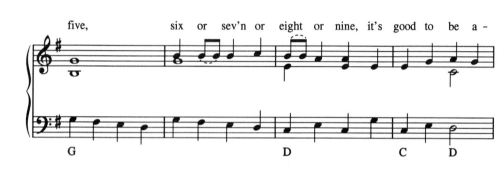

five, six or sev'n or eight or nine, it's good to be a-

G   D   C   D

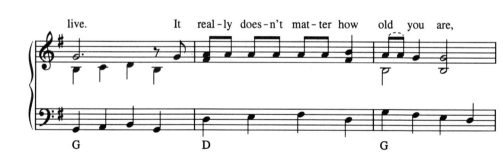

live. It real-ly does-n't mat-ter how old you are,

G   D   G

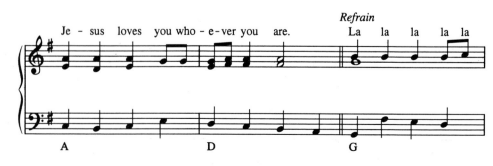

Refrain

Je - sus loves you who - e-ver you are. La la la la la

A   D   G

2. Whether you're big or whether you're small,
   or somewhere in between,
   first in the class or middle or last,
   we're all the same to him.
   It really doesn't matter how clever you are,
   Jesus loves you whoever you are.

Words: Graham Kendrick
Music: Graham Kendrick, arr. Noel Rawsthorne

The
Children's
Hymn
Book

234 Who made the corn grow?

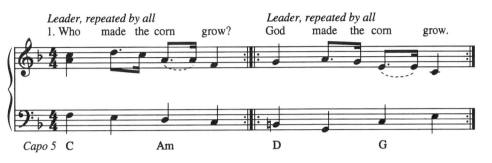

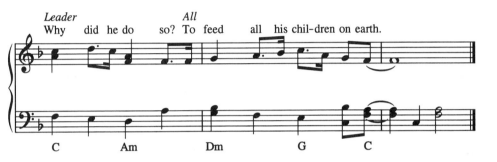

2. Who made the beans grow?
   Who made the beans grow?
   God made the beans grow.
   God made the beans grow.
   Why did he do so?
   To feed all his children on earth.

3. Who made the fruit grow?
   Who made the fruit grow?
   God made the fruit grow.
   God made the fruit grow.
   Why did he do so?
   To feed all his children on earth.

4. Who made the carrots grow?
   Who made the carrots grow?
   God made the carrots grow.
   God made the carrots grow.
   Why did he do so?
   To feed all his children on earth.

5. Who made the yams grow?
   Who made the yams grow?
   God made the yams grow.
   God made the yams grow.
   Why did he do so?
   To feed all his children on earth.

*Other verses may be improvised as
desired.*

Words: Susan Sayers
Music: Susan Sayers, arr. Noel Rawsthorne

235 Who put the colours in the rainbow?

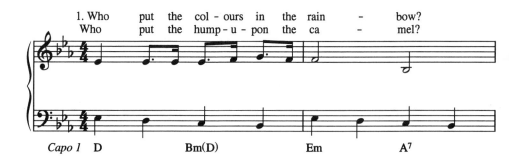

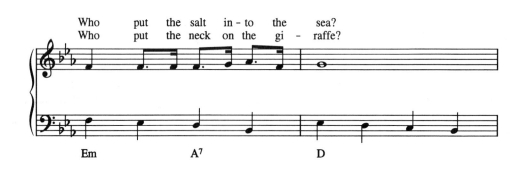

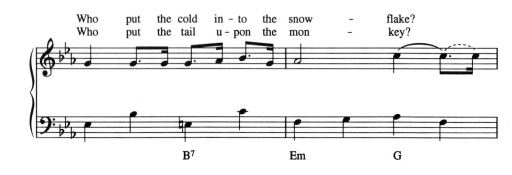

2. Who put the gold into the sunshine?
   Who put the sparkle in the stars?
   Who put the silver in the moonlight?
   Who made Earth and Mars?
   Who put the scent into the roses?
   Who taught the honey bee to dance?
   Who put the tree inside the acorn?
   It surely can't be chance!
   Who made seas and leaves and trees?
   Who made snow and winds that blow?
   Who made streams and rivers flow?
   God made all of these!

Words: Paul Booth
Music: Paul Booth, arr. Noel Rawsthorne

236 Who's the king of the jungle?

Words: unknown
Music: unknown, arr. Noel Rawsthorne

This arrangement © Copyright 1997 Kevin Mayhew Ltd.

37 With Jesus in the boat

Words: unknown
Music: unknown, arr. Noel Rawsthorne

This arrangement © Copyright 1997 Kevin Mayhew Ltd.

The
Children's
Hymn
Book

238 Yesterday, today, for ever

Yes - ter-day, to - day, for e - ver, Je - sus is the same;

all may change, but Je - sus ne - ver, glo - ry to his name!

Glo - ry to his name! Glo - ry to his name!

All may change, but Je - sus ne-ver, glo - ry to his name!

Words: unknown
Music: unknown, arr. Noel Rawsthorne

This arrangement © Copyright 1997 Kevin Mayhew Ltd.

239 You are the King of glory
Hosanna to the Son of David

Capo 5

You are the King of glo-ry, you are the Prince of peace,
you are the Lord of heav'n and earth, you're the Son of right-eous-ness!
An - gels bow down be - fore you, wor - ship and a - dore, for
you have the words of e - ter-nal life, you are Je-sus Christ the Lord! Ho-
san-na to the Son of Da-vid. Ho - san-na to the King of kings!

Glo-ry in the high-est hea - ven, for Je-sus the Mes-si - ah reigns.

C   G⁷   C   Am   Dm   G⁷   C

Words: Mavis Ford
Music: Mavis Ford, arr. Noel Rawsthorne

240 You can drink it, swim in it
Water

1. You can drink it, swim in it, cook and wash up in it,

C   G⁷   C

fish can breathe in it, what can it be? *Refrain* It's wa-ter!

G⁷   C

God has pro-vi-ded us wa-ter! Wa-ter of life.

F (Dm)   C   G⁷   C

2. It's as hard as rock,
   yet it flows down a mountain,
   and clouds drop drips of it –
   what can it be?

3. It's as light as snowflakes
   and heavy as hailstones,
   as small as dewdrops
   and big as the sea.

Words: Susan Sayers
Music: Susan Sayers, arr. Noel Rawsthorne

241 You shall go out with joy
The trees of the field

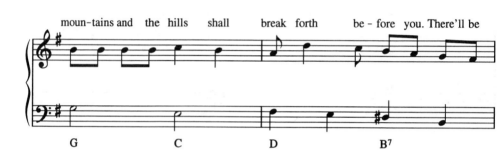

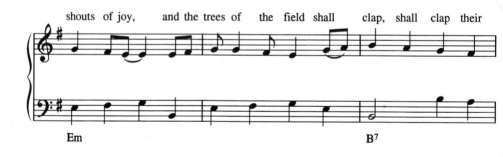

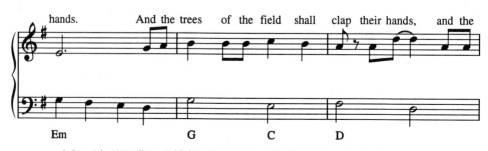

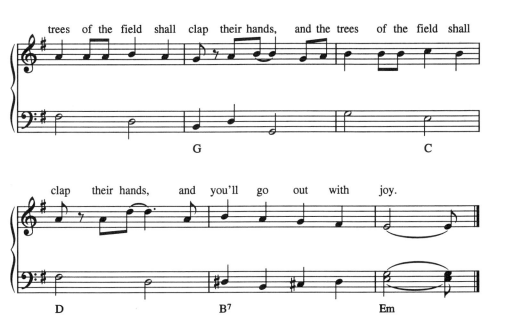

Words: Stuart Dauermann
Music: Stuart Dauermann, arr. Christopher Tambling

242 You've got to move

Moderate rock tempo

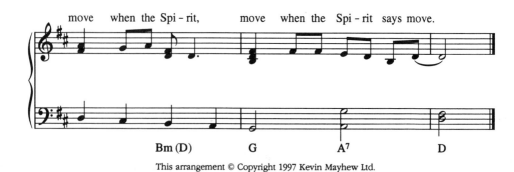

2. You've got to sing when the Spirit says sing,
   you've got to sing when the Spirit says sing,
   'cause when the Spirit says sing,
   you've got to sing when the Spirit,
   sing when the Spirit says sing.

3. You've got to clap when the Spirit says clap,
   you've got to clap when the Spirit says clap,
   'cause when the Spirit says clap,
   you've got to clap when the Spirit,
   clap when the Spirit says clap.

4. You've got to shout when the Spirit says shout,
   you've got to shout when the Spirit says shout,
   'cause when the Spirit says shout,
   you've got to shout when the Spirit,
   shout when the Spirit says shout.

5. You've got to move when the Spirit says move,
   you've got to move when the Spirit says move,
   'cause when the Spirit says move,
   you've got to move when the Spirit,
   move when the Spirit says move.

Words: traditional
Music: traditional, arr. Noel Rawsthorne

The
Children's
Hymn
Book

243 Zacchaeus was a very little man

Words: unknown
Music: unknown, arr. Noel Rawsthorne

244 Zip bam boo

Brightly

Refrain

Zip bam boo, za-ma la-ma la boo, there's free-dom in Je-sus Christ.

Capo 3   D   G   D

Zip bam boo, za-ma la-ma la boo, there's free-dom in Je-sus Christ.

A⁷

Though we hung him on a cross till he died in pain,

D   D⁷

three days la-ter he's a-live a-gain. Zip bam boo, za-ma la-ma la boo, there's

G   G⁷   D   G

free-dom in Je-sus Christ.   *Fine*   1. This Je-sus was a

D   A⁷   D   G   D

2. He'd come to share good news from God
   and show that he is Lord.
   He made folk whole who trusted him
   and took him at his word.
   He fought oppression, loved the poor,
   gave the people hope once more.
   Zip bam boo, zama lama la boo,
   there's freedom in Jesus Christ.

3. 'He's mad! He claims to be God's Son
   and give new life to men!
   Let's kill this Christ, once and for all,
   no trouble from him then!'
   'It's death then, Jesus, the cross for you!'
   Said, 'Man, that's what I came to do!'
   Zip bam boo, zama lama la boo,
   there's freedom in Jesus Christ.

Words: Sue McClellan, John Paculabo and Keith Ryecroft
Music: Sue McClellan, John Paculabo and Keith Ryecroft, arr. Norman Warren

Christmas Songs and Carols

245 Away in a manger

1. A-way in a man-ger, no crib for a bed, the
   lit-tle Lord Je-sus laid down his sweet head. The
   stars in the bright sky looked down where he lay, the
   lit-tle Lord Je-sus, a-sleep on the hay.

Capo 3

D A D B⁷ Em
A⁷ D E⁷ A
D A D B⁷ Em
A⁷ D Em A⁷ D

2. The cattle are lowing, they also adore
   the little Lord Jesus who lies in the straw.
   I love you, Lord Jesus, I know you are near
   to love and protect me, till morning is here.

3. Be near me, Lord Jesus, I ask you to stay
   close by me for ever, and love me, I pray.
   Bless all the dear children in your tender car
   prepare us for heaven, to live with you there

Words: William James Kirkpatrick
Verses 2 and 3 adapted by Michael Forster
Music: William James Kirkpatrick, arr. Alan Ridout

Verses 2 and 3 and this arrangement © Copyright 1996 Kevin Mayhew Ltd.

246 Born in the night

1. Born in the night, Ma-ry's child, a long way from your home;

Capo 3 E   C♯min (E)   A   Am   E   C♯min (E)   F♯m (A)   B⁷

com - ing in need, Ma-ry's child, born in a bor - rowed room.

E   A   F♯m (A)   B⁷   E

2. Clear shining light,
   Mary's child,
   your face lights up our way;
   light of the world,
   Mary's child,
   dawn on our darkened day.

3. Truth of our life,
   Mary's child,
   you tell us God is good;
   prove it is true,
   Mary's child,
   go to your cross of wood.

4. Hope of the world,
   Mary's child,
   you're coming soon to reign;
   King of the earth,
   Mary's child,
   walk in our streets again.

Words: Geoffrey Ainger
Music: Geoffrey Ainger, arr. Noel Rawsthorne

247 Come and join the celebration

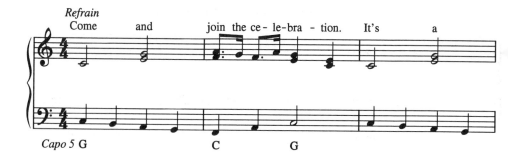

Refrain
Come and join the ce-le-bra-tion. It's a

Capo 5 G   C   G

ve - ry spe-cial day.   Come and share our ju-bi-la-tion;

C   D   G   C   G

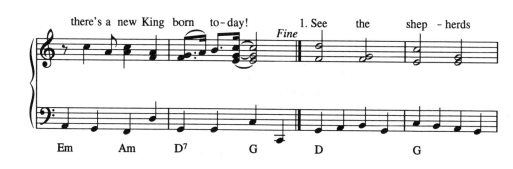

there's a new King born to-day!   1. See the shep - herds

Fine

Em   Am   D7   G   D   G

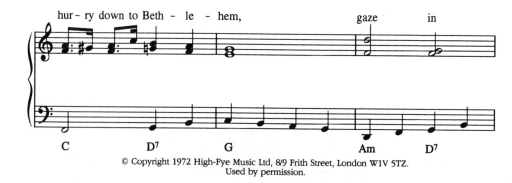

hur - ry down to Beth - le - hem,   gaze in

C   D7   G   Am   D7

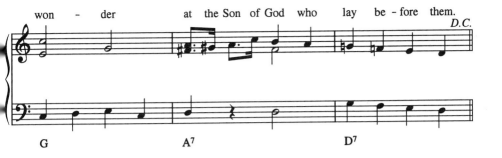

2. Wise men journey,
led to worship by a star,
kneel in homage,
bringing precious gifts from lands afar. So:

3. 'God is with us,'
round the world the message bring.
He is with us,
'Welcome,' all the bells on earth are pealing.

Words: Valerie Collison
Music: Valerie Collison, arr. Noel Rawsthorne

248 Come, they told me
The little drummer boy

rum-pum-pum-pum! Rum-pum-pum-pum! Rum-pum-pum-pum!

G   D   A

So,   to   ho-nour him, pah - rum-pum-pum-pum!

D   A   D

when we come.   D.S.

last time repeat & fade

A   D

2. Baby Jesus, pah-rum-pum-pum-pum!
   I am a poor child too, pah-rum-pum-pum-pum!
   I have no gift to bring, pah-rum-pum-pum-pum!
   that's fit to give a King, pah-rum-pum-pum-pum!
   Rum-pum-pum-pum! Rum-pum-pum-pum!
   Shall I play for you, pah-rum-pum-pum-pum!
   on my drum?

3. Mary nodded, pah-rum-pum-pum-pum!
   The ox and lamb kept time, pah-rum-pum-pum-pum!
   I played my drum for him, pah-rum-pum-pum-pum!
   I played my best for him, pah-rum-pum-pum-pum!
   Rum-pum-pum-pum! Rum-pum-pum-pum!
   Then he smiled at me, pah-rum-pum-pum-pum!
   me and my drum.

Words: Katherine K. Davis
Music: Katherine K. Davis, arr. Noel Rawsthorne

249 Everyone's a Christmas baby

With a swing

Refrain

Ev - 'ry-one's a Christ-mas ba - by, ev - 'ry - one's a Christ-mas child.

Capo 5 G   D⁷

We've got Je - sus as a broth - er, we've got Ma - ry as a mo - ther,

G   C   A

yes, ev - 'ry - one's a Christ - mas child.

Fine

D   G

1. Ev - 'ry new - born hu - man child is a sign of hope and joy, and

C

God is smil-ing up at us from ev-'ry girl and boy. Yes!

D.C.

D⁷   G   E   Am   D⁷   G

2. Christmas comes on ev'ry day,
   and in ev'ry kind of place,
   for each new child that's born on earth
   reveals God's love and grace. Yes!

3. Life and hope begin anew
   when another child is born,
   and ev'ry morning that we awake
   is like a new world's dawn. Yes!

Words: Sarah Forth
Music: Noel Rawsthorne

250 Go, tell it on the mountain

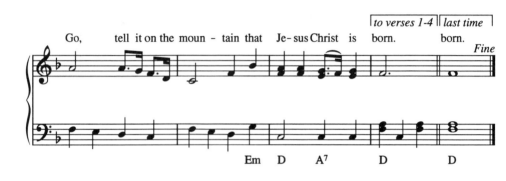

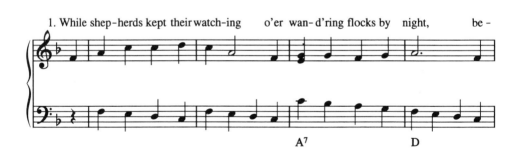

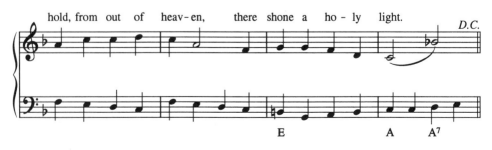

2. And lo, when they had seen it,
   they all bowed down and prayed;
   they travelled on together
   to where the babe was laid.

3. When first I was a seeker,
   I sought both night and day;
   I asked the Lord to help me
   and he showed me the way.

4. He set me as a watchman
   upon the city wall,
   and if I am a Christian,
   I am the least of all.

Words: Spiritual
Music: Spiritual, arr. Noel Rawsthorne

251 God was born on earth
Never mind the sheep, look for the baby

Allegretto

1. God was born on earth, a

Capo 3 D · A⁷

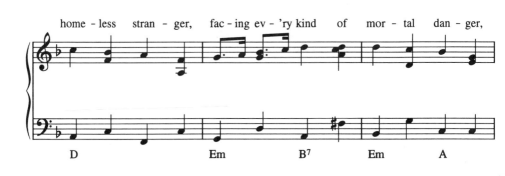

home - less stran - ger, fac - ing ev - 'ry kind of mor - tal dan - ger,

D · Em · B⁷ · Em · A

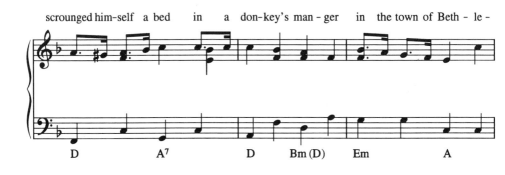

scrounged him-self a bed in a don-key's man - ger in the town of Beth - le -

D · A⁷ · D · Bm (D) · Em · A

hem.

Refrain

Ne - ver mind the sheep, look for the ba - by,

D · A · Dm · A · F (Dm) · Dm

2. Shepherds in the fields with sheep to care for,
   angels said, 'What are you sitting there for?
   Never mind the questions, the whys and wherefores,
   get along to Bethlehem!'

3. 'Never mind the sheep, look for the baby,
   he's the one to watch, I don't mean maybe.
   If you want to share in this special day, be
   sure to go to Bethlehem.'

4. So they left the sheep and went out looking,
   eager to find out what God had cooking,
   found a classic problem of overbooking
   in the town of Bethlehem.

5. Jesus doesn't put on airs and graces,
   Likes to be in unexpected places,
   comes to us in smiles and warm embraces,
   as he did at Bethlehem.

Words: Michael Forster
Music: Andrew Gant

252 Hee, haw! Hee, haw!
The donkey's Christmas carol

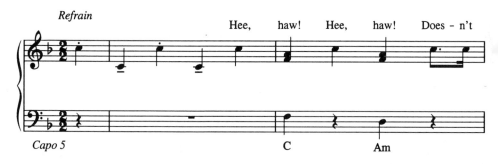

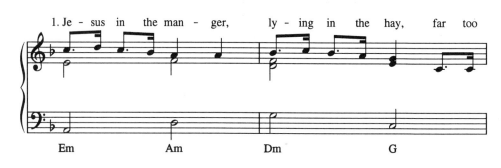

2. After all that journey,
   with my heavy load,
   did I ever once complain about the dreadful road?
   I can cope with backache,
   and these swollen feet.
   All I ask is some respect, and one square meal to eat.

3. 'Be prepared,' I told them,
   'better book ahead.'
   Joseph said, 'Don't be an ass,' and took a chance instead.
   Now they've pinched my bedroom,
   people are so rude!
   I can cope with that, but not a baby in my food!

Words: Michael Forster
Music: Noel Rawsthorne

253 I wonder as I wander

2. When Mary birthed Jesus, 'twas in a cow's stall
   with wise men and farmers and shepherds and all.
   But high from God's heaven a star's light did fall,
   and the promise of ages it did then recall.

3. If Jesus had wanted for any wee thing,
   a star in the sky or a bird on the wing,
   or all of God's angels in heav'n for to sing,
   he surely could have it, 'cause he was the King.

Words: John Jacob Niles
Music: John Jacob Niles, arr. Alan Ridout

254 Joy to the world

Joy to the earth! The Saviour reigns;
let us our songs employ;
while fields and floods, rocks, hills and plains
repeat the sounding joy,
repeat the sounding joy,
repeat, repeat the sounding joy.

3. He rules the world with truth and grace,
and makes the nations prove
the glories of his righteousness,
and wonders of his love,
and wonders of his love,
and wonders, wonders of his love.

Words: Isaac Watts, alt.
Music: George Frideric Handel, arr. Noel Rawsthorne

255 Light a flame

With energy

Refrain

1. From hea-ven's splen - dour he comes to earth,

Am   B   E   Am   E

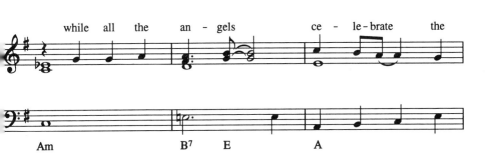

while all the an - gels ce - le - brate the

Am   B⁷   E   A

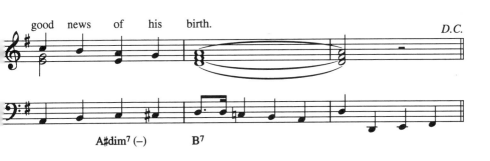

good news of his birth.   *D.C.*

A♯dim⁷ (–)   B⁷

2. We too exalt you,
   our glorious King:
   Jesus our Saviour
   paid the price to take away our sin.

Words: Mick Gisbey
Music: Mick Gisbey, arr. Noel Rawsthorne

The
Children's
Hymn
Book

256 Mary had a baby

1. Ma-ry had a ba-by, yes, Lord. Ma-ry had a ba-by,

Capo 5 C   Am   Dm   G⁷   C   Am

yes, my Lord. Ma-ry had a ba-by, yes, Lord. And

D⁷   G⁷   C   Am   F(Dm)   G⁷

God be-came a hu-man be-ing just like me.

C   D⁷   G⁷   C

2. What did she name him?

3. Mary named him Jesus.

4. Where was he born?

5. Born in a stable!

6. Where did she lay him?

7. Laid him in a manger.

This song may be sung between a leader ('Mary had a baby') and All ('yes, Lord').

Words: Spiritual, alt.
Music: Spiritual, arr. Colin Hand

257 Mary said to Joseph
There wasn't any room at the inn

Gently

1. Ma - ry said to Jo - seph, 'Let's find a place to stay, for it's

G   Am   D⁷   G

much too cold to sleep out-side with a ba - by on the way!'

Em   Bm (D)   A⁷   D

Refrain

There was - n't a - ny room at the inn. There was-n't a-ny

G   E   Am   D

room at the inn. They could-n't find a bed for a

G   E   Am

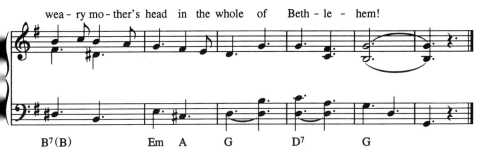

wea - ry mo - ther's head in the whole of Beth - le - hem!

B7(B)   Em   A   G   D7   G

2. Joseph said to Mary,
   'I hope we'll find a place,
   but the town is full of visitors
   and there's not a lot of space.'

3. Then they found a stable,
   a simple little shed,
   and the Saviour of the world was born
   with a manger for his bed!

Words: Michael Forster
Music: Christopher Tambling

258 O come, all ye faithful

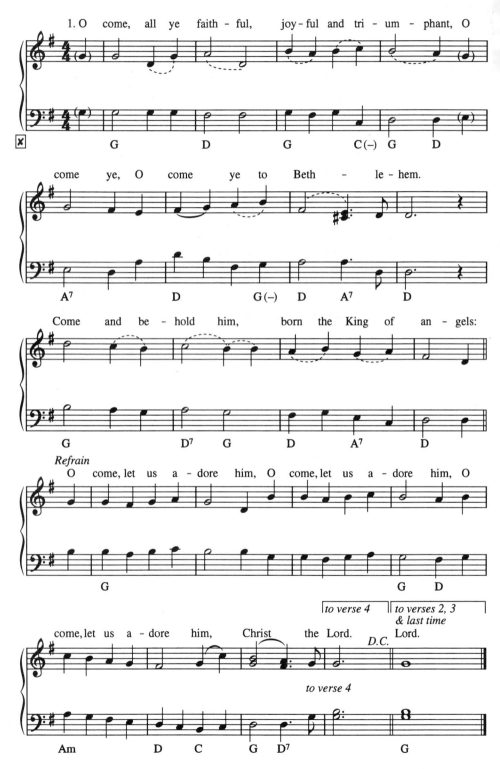

2. God of God,
   Light of Light,
   lo, he abhors not the virgin's womb;
   Very God,
   begotten, not created:

3. Sing, choirs of angels,
   sing in exultation,
   sing, all ye citizens of heav'n above;
   glory to God
   in the highest:

4. Yea, Lord, we greet thee,
   born this happy morning,
   Jesu, to thee be glory giv'n;
   Word of the Father,
   now in flesh appearing:

Words: possibly by John Francis Wade, trans. Frederick Oakeley and others
Music: possibly by John Francis Wade, arr. Alan Ridout

259 O little town of Bethlehem

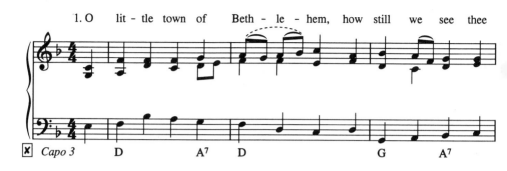

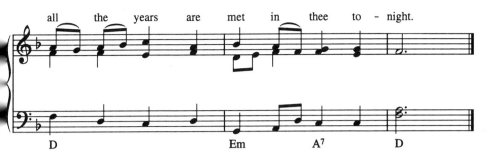

all   the   years   are   met   in   thee   to - night.

2. For Christ is born of Mary;
   and, gathered all above,
   while mortals sleep, the angels keep
   their watch of wond'ring love;
   O morning stars, together
   proclaim the holy birth,
   and praises sing to God the King,
   and peace upon the earth.

3. How silently, how silently,
   the wondrous gift is giv'n!
   So God imparts to human hearts
   the blessings of his heav'n.
   No ear may hear his coming;
   but in this world of sin,
   where meek souls will receive him, still
   the dear Christ enters in.

4. O holy child of Bethlehem,
   descend to us, we pray;
   cast out our sin and enter in,
   be born in us today.
   We hear the Christmas angels
   the great glad tidings tell:
   O come to us, abide with us,
   our Lord Emmanuel.

Words: Phillips Brooks, alt.
Music: traditional English melody arr. by Ralph Vaughan Williams,
adapted by Guthrie Foote

260 Once in royal David's city

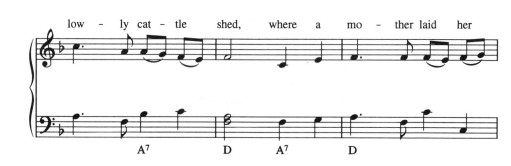

2. He came down to earth from heaven,
   who is God and Lord of all,
   and his shelter was a stable,
   and his cradle was a stall;
   with the humble, poor and lowly,
   lived on earth our Saviour holy.

3. And through all his wondrous childhood,
   day by day like us he grew;
   he was little, weak and helpless,
   tears and smiles like us he knew;
   and he feeleth for our sadness,
   and he shareth in our gladness.

4. Still, among the poor and lowly,
   hope in Christ is brought to birth,
   with the promise of salvation
   for the nations of the earth;
   still in him our life is found,
   and our hope of heav'n is crowned.

5. And our eyes at last shall see him,
   through his own redeeming love,
   for that child, so dear and gentle,
   is our Lord in heav'n above;
   and he leads his children on
   to the place where he is gone.

Words: verses 1, 2, 3 and 5: Cecil Frances Alexander
verse 4: Michael Forster
Music: Henry John Gauntlett, arr. Alan Ridout

261 See him lying on a bed of straw
Calypso carol

1. See him ly - ing on a bed of straw, a draugh-ty sta - ble with an

D   Em   A⁷

o - pen door, Ma - ry cra - dl- ing the babe she bore: the

D   Em

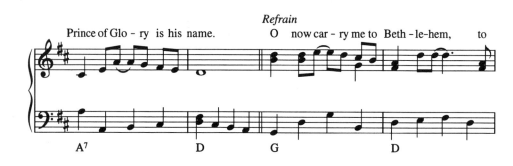

Prince of Glo - ry is his name. *Refrain* O now car - ry me to Beth - le-hem, to

A⁷   D G D

see the Lord of love a-gain: just as poor as was the

A⁷   D

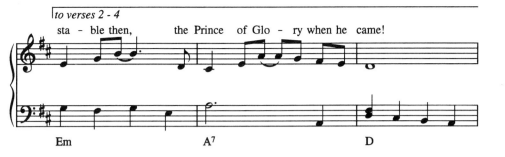

to verses 2 - 4

sta - ble then, the Prince of Glo - ry when he came!

Em   A⁷   D

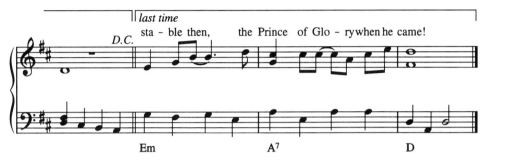

last time

D.C. sta - ble then, the Prince of Glo - ry when he came!

Em   A⁷   D

2. Star of silver, sweep across the skies,
   show where Jesus in a manger lies;
   shepherds, swiftly from your stupor rise
   to see the Saviour of the world!

3. Angels, sing again the song you sang,
   sing the story of God's gracious plan,
   sing that Bethl'em's little baby can
   be the Saviour of us all.

4. Mine are riches from your poverty;
   from your innocence, eternity;
   mine, forgiveness by your death for me,
   child of sorrow for my joy.

Words: Michael Perry
Music: Michael Perry, arr. Noel Rawsthorne

262 Silent night

2. Silent night, holy night.
   Shepherds quake at the sight,
   glories stream from heaven afar,
   heav'nly hosts sing alleluia:
   Christ the Saviour is born,
   Christ the Saviour is born.

3. Silent night, holy night.
   Son of God, love's pure light,
   radiance beams from thy holy face,
   with the dawn of redeeming grace:
   Jesus, Lord, at thy birth,
   Jesus, Lord, at thy birth.

Words: Joseph Mohr, trans. John Freeman Young
Music: Franz Grüber, arr. Alan Ridout

263 Sing lullaby

2. Sing lullaby!
   Lullaby baby, now a-sleeping,
   sing lullaby!
   Hush, do not wake the infant King.
   Soon will come sorrow with the morning,
   soon will come bitter grief and weeping:
   sing lullaby!

3. Sing lullaby!
   Lullaby baby, now a-dozing,
   sing lullaby!
   Hush, do not wake the infant King.
   Soon comes the cross, the nails, the piercing,
   then in the grave at last reposing:
   sing lullaby!

4. Sing lullaby!
   Lullaby! is the babe awaking?
   Sing lullaby!
   Hush, do not stir the infant King,
   dreaming of Easter, gladsome morning,
   conquering death, its bondage breaking:
   sing lullaby!

Words: Sabine Baring-Gould
Music: traditional Basque Noël, arr. Noel Rawsthorne

264 The angel Gabriel from heaven came

2. 'For known a blessèd mother thou shalt be.
All generations laud and honour thee.
Thy Son shall be Emmanuel, by seers foretold,
most highly favoured lady.' Gloria!

3. Then gentle Mary meekly bowed her head.
'To me be as it pleaseth God,' she said.
'My soul shall laud and magnify his holy name.'
Most highly favoured lady. Gloria!

4. Of her, Emmanuel the Christ was born
in Bethlehem, all on a Christmas morn;
and Christian folk throughout the world will ever say:
'Most highly favoured lady.' Gloria!

Words: Sabine Baring-Gould
Music: traditional Basque melody, arr. Alan Ridout

265 The first nowell

2. They looked up and saw a star
   shining in the east, beyond them far,
   and to the earth it gave great light,
   and so it continued both day and night.

3. And by the light of that same star,
   three wise men came from country far;
   to seek for a king was their intent,
   and to follow the star wherever it went.

4. This star drew nigh to the north-west,
   o'er Bethlehem it took its rest,
   and there it did both stop and stay
   right over the place where Jesus lay.

5. Then entered in those wise men three,
   full rev'rently upon their knee,
   and offered there, in his presence,
   their gold and myrrh and frankincense.

6. Then let us all with one accord
   sing praises to our heavenly Lord,
   that hath made heav'n and earth of naught,
   and with his blood mankind hath bought.

Words: from William Sandys' *Christmas Carols Ancient and Modern*
Music: traditional English melody, arr. Alan Ridout

266 The holly and the ivy

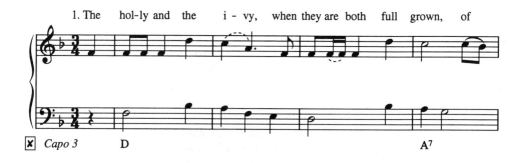

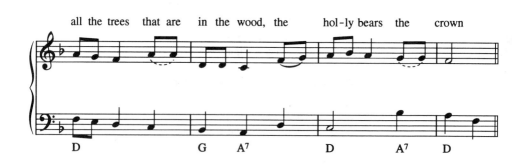

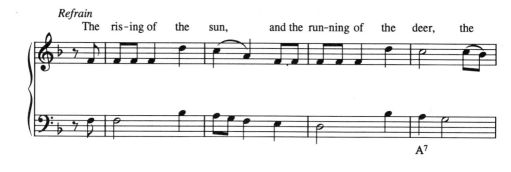

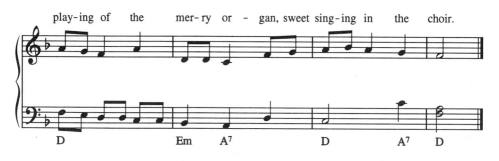

2. The holly bears a blossom
   as white as the lily flow'r,
   and Mary bore sweet Jesus Christ
   to be our sweet Saviour.

3. The holly bears a berry
   as red as any blood,
   and Mary bore sweet Jesus Christ
   to do poor sinners good.

4. The holly bears a prickle
   as sharp as any thorn,
   and Mary bore sweet Jesus Christ
   on Christmas day in the morn.

5. The holly bears a bark
   as bitter as any gall,
   and Mary bore sweet Jesus Christ
   for to redeem us all.

6. The holly and the ivy,
   when they are both full grown,
   of all the trees that are in the wood
   the holly bears the crown.

Words: traditional English carol
Music: traditional English melody, arr. Alan Ridout

267 There's a star in the east
Rise up, shepherd, and follow

2. If you take good heed of the angel's words,
   rise up, shepherd, and follow,
   you'll leave your flocks, you'll forget your herds,
   rise up, shepherd, and follow.

Words: Spiritual
Music: Spiritual, arr. Alan Ridout

268 We three kings of Orient are

2. Born a King on Bethlehem plain,
gold I bring to crown him again,
King for ever, ceasing never
over us all to reign.

3. Frankincense to offer have I,
incense owns a Deity nigh,
prayer and praising gladly raising,
worship him, God most high.

4. Myrrh is mine, its bitter perfume
breathes a life of gathering gloom;
sorrowing, sighing, bleeding, dying,
sealed in the stone-cold tomb.

5. Glorious now, behold him arise,
King and God and sacrifice;
alleluia, alleluia,
earth to heav'n replies.

Words: John Henry Hopkins
Music: John Henry Hopkins, arr. Alan Ridout

269 We wish you a merry Christmas

2. Now bring us some figgy pudding,
   now bring us some figgy pudding,
   now bring us some figgy pudding,
   and bring some out here.

3. We all like figgy pudding,
   we all like figgy pudding,
   we all like figgy pudding,
   so bring some out here.

4. We won't go until we've got some,
   we won't go until we've got some,
   we won't go until we've got some,
   so bring some out here.

Words: traditional English
Music: traditional English carol, arr. Alan Ridout

270 While shepherds watched

1. While shep - herds watched their flocks by night, all seat - ed on the

Capo 5   C   Am (C)   F (Dm)   C   D⁷

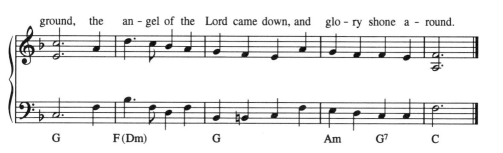

ground, the an - gel of the Lord came down, and glo - ry shone a - round.

G   F (Dm)   G   Am   G⁷   C

2. 'Fear not,' said he (for mighty dread
   had seized their trouble mind);
   'glad tidings of great joy I bring
   to you and all mankind.

3. 'To you, in David's town this day,
   is born, of David's line,
   a Saviour who is Christ the Lord;
   and this shall be the sign:

4. 'The heav'nly babe you there shall find
   to human view displayed,
   all meanly wrapped in swathing bands
   and in a manger laid.'

5. Thus spake the seraph, and forthwith
   appeared a shining throng
   of angels praising God, who thus
   addressed their joyful song:

6. 'All glory be to God on high
   and to the earth be peace;
   good will from heav'n to all the world
   begin and never cease.'

Words: Nahum Tate
Music: from Thomas Este's *Psalter*, arr. Alan Ridout

Indexes

Index of Composers
and Sources of Music

Adkins, Donna 46
Ainger, Geoffrey 246
Anderson, Mike 58
Andrew, Diane Davis 193
Appleford, Patrick 145, 161

Bailey, Judy 101
Ballantine, John 61
Batya, Naomi 132
Bell, John L. 226
Berthier, Jacques 125, 134, 162, 215
Bilbrough, Dave 4
Booth, Paul 228, 235
Brabazon, Ruth 18
Brethorst, Leona von 106
Burn, Mike 100

Carter, Sydney 95, 96, 166, 182, 194,
    229
Coelho, Terrye 45
Collison, Valerie 247
Conty, Sophie 132
Cox, S.E. 83
Craig, Ian D. 71, 147

Daniels, Danny 60
Dauermann, Stuart 241
Davis, Katherine K. 248
Dunn, Fred 130
Dyer, Max 107

Elliott, Winifred 25
Espinosa, Eddie 29
Este, Thomas 270
Evans, David J. 20

Filitz, Friedrich 144
Fishel, Donald 16
Fitzpatrick, Gerard 117, 135
Foote, Guthrie 171, 259
Ford, Mavis 239

Gammon, Bev 38
Gant, Andrew 67, 157, 189, 206, 251
Garrard, Stuart 43
Garrett, Les 211
Gauntlett, Henry John 260
Geistliche Kirchengesäng 6
Gillard, Richard 27
Gillman, Bob 22
Gisbey, Mick 216, 255
Grüber, Franz 262

Handel, George Frideric 254
Hanson, B.C. 196

Hardwick, John 156
Harvey, Jancis 3
Hayward, Rob 109
Hewer, Jenny 44
Hind, David 129
Hopkins, John Henry 268
Horsley, William 204
Howard, Brian 114
Hubbard, Richard 77
Hutchinson, Gill 122, 191

Johnson, Orien 85

Kendrick, Graham 36, 52, 124, 148,
    197, 233
Kirkpatrick, William James 245

Lafferty, Karen 40, 184
Landry, Carey 1
Larsson, John 202
Leavers, Greg 53, 128
Lloyd, Richard 42, 111

Mann, Robin 48
Markland, Gerard 37, 104
Marks-Smirchich, Doug 9
Maule, Graham 226
Mawby, Colin 143
Mayhew, Kevin 14, 87, 173, 183, 185
McClellan, Sue 33, 244
Middleton, Kathleen 68
Mitchell, Hugh 92
Moore, Andrew 141
Morgan, Janet 56
Morgan, Patricia 35
Morstad, David 51

Nazareth, Aniceto 4, 74, 142,
Niles, John Jacob 253

Owens, Carol 65
Owens, Jimmy 31, 175

Paculabo, John 33, 244
Parry, Hubert 160
Patten, James 41, 94
Perry, Michael 261
Pinnock, Alan 79
Pond, Joanne 158
Potter, Doreen 139
Price, Alan J. 21, 112, 118, 150, 214
Psalter 270

Rawsthorne, Noel 97, 188, 203, 224,
    249, 252

Rose, Peter 232
Russell, Eileen 84
Ryecroft, Keith 33, 244

Sayers, Susan 11, 28, 47, 49, 63, 97,
    99, 115, 131, 138, 155, 178, 192,
    195, 208, 209, 213, 230, 234, 240
Schulz, Johann 223
Schutte, Dan 102
Setchell, Martin 66, 151
Sister Madeleine 50
Smale, Ian 105, 108, 149, 154, 225
Smith, Henry 57
Spiritual 8, 113, 119, 133, 250, 256,
    267
Strover, Christian 78

Tambling, Christopher 10, 26, 39,
    69, 70, 73, 81, 110, 120, 121, 127,
    137, 140, 165, 170, 176, 190, 199,
    201, 207, 220, 227, 257
Tarner, Evelyn 180
Temple, Sebastian 13, 152
Traditional American melody 96, 205
Traditional Basque melody 264
Traditional Caribbean melody 167
Traditional English carol 269
Traditional English melody 15, 15a,
    59, 62, 116, 126, 221, 259, 265, 266
Traditional Hebrew melody 186
Traditional Irish melody 90, 146, 153
Traditional Italian melody 136
Traditional Jamaican melody 139
Traditional melody 7, 32, 55, 64, 82,
    98, 159, 163, 212, 222, 242
Traditional Peruvian melody 61
Traditional Scottish melody 54, 89,
    171
Traditional South African melody
    218
Traditional Welsh melody 187
Turner, Roy 12
Tuttle, Carl 91

Vaughan Williams, Ralph 259
Vissing, Rosalie 5

Wade, John Francis 258
Warren, Norman 103
Westcott, Graham 210
White, Estelle 30, 179, 217
Wiener, Julian 168
Wiseman, Herbert 171

Index of Authors, Translators
and Sources of Words

Adkins, Donna 46
Ainger, Geoffrey 246
Alexander, Cecil Frances 15, 204, 260
Anderson, Mike 58
Andrew, Diane Davis 193
Appleford, Patrick 145, 161

Bailey, Judy 101
Baring-Gould, Sabine 263, 264
Batya, Naomi 132
Bell, John L. 226
Bilbrough, Dave 4
Billington, Sandra Joan 186
Booth, Paul 228, 235
Brethorst, Leona von 106
Brooks, Phillips 259
Brown, Ruth 171
Burn, Mike 100

Campbell, James Montgomery 223
Carter, Sydney 95, 96, 166, 182, 194, 229
Christmas Carols 265
Claudius, Matthias 223
Cockett, Michael 14, 50
Coelho, Terrye 45
Collison, Valerie 247
Conlon, Ann 232
Conty, Sophie 132
Cox, S.E. 83
Craig, Ian D. 71, 147

Daniels, Danny 60
Dauermann, Stuart 241
Davidson, Dave 203
Davis, Katherine K. 248
Draper, William Henry 6
Dunn, Fred 130
Dyer, Max 107

Elliott, Winifred 25
Espinosa, Eddie 29
Evans, David J. 20

Farjeon, Eleanor 153
Farrow, Richard 189
Fishel, Donald 16
Fitzpatrick, Gerard 117
Ford, Mavis 239
Forster, Michael 10, 26, 39, 41, 59, 62, 69, 70, 73, 81, 89, 90, 103, 110, 120, 121, 126, 127, 137, 140, 144, 159, 160, 165, 170, 176, 187, 190, 199, 201, 206, 207, 220, 227, 245, 251, 252, 257, 260
Forth, Sarah 249

Gammon, Bev 38
Garrard, Stuart 43
Garrett, Les 211
Gillard, Richard 27
Gillman, Bob 22
Gisbey, Mick 216, 255
Gowans, John 202

Hanson, B.C. 196
Hardwick, John 156
Harvey, Jancis 3
Hayward, Rob 109
Hewer, Jenny 44
Hind, David 129
Holloway, Jean 32, 54
Hopkins, John Henry 268
Howard, Brian 114
Hubbard, Richard 77
Hutchinson, Gill 122, 191

Johnson, Orien 85

Kaan, Fred 139, 222
Ken, Thomas 175
Kendrick, Graham 36, 52, 124, 148, 197, 233
Kirkpatrick, William James 245
Kontakion 185

Lafferty, Karen 40, 184
Landry, Carey 1
Leavers, Greg 53, 128
Lundy, Damian 136, 198

McClellan, Sue 33, 244
Mann, Robin 48
Markland, Gerard 37, 104
Marks-Smirchich, Doug 9
Marshall-Taylor, Geoffrey 193
Maule, Graham 226
Mayhew, Kevin 87, 173, 183
Mee, Susan 221
Middleton, Kathleen 68
Mitchell, Hugh 92
Mohr, Joseph 262
Morgan, Janet 56
Morgan, Patricia 35
Morstad, David 51

Nazareth, Aniceto 24, 74, 142
Newport, Doreen 210
Niles, John Jacob 253
Nyberg, Anders 218

Oakeley, Frederick 258
Owens, Carol 65
Owens, Jimmy 31

Paculabo, John 33, 244
Perry, Michael 261
Pinnock, Alan 79
Pond, Joanne 158
Price, Alan J. 21, 118, 150, 214

Rattle, H.W. 123
Russell, Eileen 84
Ryberg, Barbara 18
Ryecroft, Keith 33, 244

Sandys, William 265
Sayers, Susan 11, 28, 47, 49, 63, 97, 99, 115, 131, 138, 155, 178, 192, 195, 208, 209, 213, 230, 234
Schutte, Dan 102
Smale, Ian 105, 108, 149, 154, 225
Smith, Henry 57
Somerville, Caroline 64
Spiritual 8, 113, 119, 133, 250, 256, 267
Strover, Christian 78
Struther, Jan 146

Taizé Community 162, 215
Tarner, Evelyn 180
Tate, Nahum 270
Temple, Sebastian 13, 152
Traditional 7, 23, 55, 61, 75, 82, 98, 103, 125, 135, 142, 143, 163, 167, 168, 181, 212, 218, 242, 266, 269
Turner, Roy 12
Tuttle, Carl 91

Vissing, Rosalie 5

Wade, John Francis 258
Wallace, W.L. 42, 66, 67, 94, 111, 116, 141, 151, 157, 188, 219
Watts, Isaac 254
White, Estelle 30, 179, 217
Wilde, Christina 205, 224

Young, John Freeman 262

Index of Uses

CHRISTIAN THEMES

CREATION

All creatures of our God and King	6
All the nations of the earth	14
All things bright and beautiful	15
Boisterous, buzzing, barking things	25
Caterpillar, caterpillar	28
'Cheep!' said the sparrow	30
Fishes of the ocean	49
God turned darkness into light	70
Goliath was big and Goliath was strong	73
Great indeed are your works	74
He gave me eyes so I could see	79
I am cold, I am ice	94
I feel spring in the air today	97
If I were an astronaut	115
Laudato sii	136
Let the mountains dance and sing	138
Morning has broken	153
Over the earth is a mat of green	171
Push, little seed	178
Thank you for the summer morning	192
The bell of creation	194
The duck goes 'Quack'	196
There's a seed	208
Think of a world without any flowers	210
This world you have made	213
We are one family together	219
We can plough and dig the land	220
When God made the garden of creation	228
When your Father made the world	232
Who put the colours in the rainbow?	235
You can drink it, swim in it	240

CELEBRATION OF LIFE

All creatures of our God and King	6
All of the people	11
Boisterous, buzzing, barking things	25
'Cheep!' said the sparrow	30
Come on and celebrate	35
Do you ever wish you could fly	39
Every minute of every day	43
Fishes of the ocean	49
From my knees to my nose	53
God's not dead	72
Great indeed are your works	74
Have you heard the raindrops	78
He gave me eyes so I could see	79
He's got the whole world in his hand	82
Hey, now, everybody sing	85
I danced in the morning	96
I feel spring in the air today	97

I will wave my hands	108
I'm glad I'm alive	111
If I were a butterfly	114
If I were an astronaut	115
Jesus calls us to a party	120
Jesus put this song into our hearts	124
Jesus, you love me	129
Laudato sii	136
Life for the poor was hard and tough	140
Life is for living now	141
Morning has broken	153
My mouth was made for worship	154
Push, little seed	178
Sing praise to God	188
Thank you for the summer morning	192
The bell of creation	194
The clock tells the story of time	195
Think of a world without any flowers	210
Whether you're one	233
You've got to move	242
Zip bam boo	244

NEW LIFE/NEW BEGINNINGS

A butterfly, an Easter egg	1
All of the creatures God had made	10
All over the world	12
And everyone beneath the vine and fig tree	17
Caterpillar, caterpillar	28
Every minute of every day	43
Father welcomes all his children	48
Follow me	50
God sends a rainbow	69
Have you heard the raindrops	78
I danced in the morning	96
I feel spring in the air today	97
Morning has broken	53
O Lord, all the world belongs to you	161
Rise and shine	181
The voice from the bush	199
There's a rainbow in the sky	207
This is the day	211
Waiting for your Spirit	216
We can plough and dig the land	220
We have a King who rides a donkey	222

MYSTERY

Be still, for the presence of the Lord	20
Enter the darkness	42
God is the centre and the circle	67
In the first stage of seeking	116
Let love be real	137
Sing glory to God	187
The bell of creation	194
We can plough and dig the land	220
What kind of man was this	227

TRINITY

Glory and honour to God in the highest	59
Glory to God, to God in the height	62
God is the centre and the circle	67
Lord, the light of your love	148
Sing glory to God	187

GRACE AND PROVIDENCE

All over the world	12
All the nations of the earth	14
All things bright and beautiful	15
Anytime, anywhere	18
Boisterous, buzzing, barking things	25
'Cheep!' said the sparrow	30
Clap your hands and sing this song	32
Do not be afraid	37
Every minute of every day	43
Father, I place into your hands	44
Father welcomes all his children	48
Fishes of the ocean	49
From heaven you came	52
From my knees to my nose	53
Give thanks to the Lord	56
God sends a rainbow	69
God turned darkness into light	70
God's love is deeper	71
Have you heard the raindrops	78
He gave me eyes so I could see	79
He's got the whole world in his hand	82
He's the same today	83
Holy God	87
How did Moses cross the Red Sea?	92
I come like a beggar	95
I gotta home in gloryland	98
I have a friend	99
Jesus calls us to a party	120
Jesus, you love me	129
Let the mountains dance and sing	138
Life for the poor was hard and tough	140
Lord Jesus Christ	145
Lord of all hopefulness	146
Oh! Oh! Oh! how good is the Lord	164
One hundred and fifty-three!	165
Over the earth is a mat of green	171
Push, little seed	178
Seek ye first the kingdom of God	184
Stand on the corner of the street	189
The Spirit lives to set us free	198
There are hundreds of sparrows	202
There's a rainbow in the sky	207
There's a seed	208
This is the day	211
This little light of mine	212

his world you have made	213	
Walk with me, O my Lord	217	
We are marching in the light of God	218	
We can plough and dig the land	220	
We thank God for the harvest	224	
What kind of man was this	227	
When God made the garden of creation	228	
When your Father made the world	232	
Who made the corn grow?	234	
You can drink it, swim in it	240	

LOVE

A new commandment	2
Every minute of every day	43
God our Father gave us life	68
God sends a rainbow	69
God's love is deeper	71
I'm black, I'm white, I'm short, I'm tall	110
I've got peace like a river	113
In the upper room	117
Jesus had all kinds of friends	121
Jesus' love is very wonderful	123
Joy to the world	254
Just imagine	131
Let love be real	137
Love is like a circle	151
Make me a channel of your peace	152
O Lord, all the world belongs to you	161
Over the earth is a mat of green	171
Said Judas to Mary	182
Sing praise to God	188
The world is full of smelly feet	201
There's a great big world out there	206
We thank God for the harvest	224
What kind of man was this	227
When God made the garden of creation	228

HOPE AND JOY

A butterfly, an Easter egg	1
All the nations of the earth	14
And everyone beneath the vine and fig tree	17
Colours of day	33
Come into his presence	34
Come on and celebrate	35
Each of us is a living stone	41
Everyone's a Christmas baby	249
Give me joy in my heart	55
God sends a rainbow	69
God's love is deeper	71
Ho, ho, ho, hosanna	86
I gotta home in gloryland	98
I will click my fingers	105
I will enter his gates	106
I will sing, I will sing	107
I'm accepted, I'm forgiven	109
I've got peace like a river	13
Jesus put this song into our hearts	124
Joy to the world	254
Lord of all hopefulness	146

Lord, the light of your love	148
Make me a channel of your peace	152
Morning has broken	153
Not every day	157
O when the saint go marching in	163
Oh! Oh! Oh! how good is the Lord	164
Peace is flowing like a river	172
Peace, perfect peace is the gift	173
Rejoice in the Lord always	180
Rise and shine	181
The bell of creation	194
The voice from the bush	199
There's a rainbow in the sky	207
This is the day	211
Wait for the Lord	215
We have a King who rides a donkey	222
We're going to shine like the sun	226
When the Spirit of the Lord	231
You shall go out with joy	241
Zip bam boo	244

FAITH, TRUST AND COMMITMENT

A still small voice	3
Abba, Father, let me be	4
All of the creatures God had made	10
All of the people	11
Anytime, anywhere	18
Be still and know	19
Be the centre of my life	21
Do not be afraid	37
Don't build your house on the sandy land	40
Each of us is a living stone	41
Father, I place into your hands	44
Follow me	50
From heaven you came	52
God has spoken	66
God sends a rainbow	69
Great indeed are your works	74
Hang on	77
I come like a beggar	95
I danced in the morning	96
I gotta home in gloryland	98
I love to be with you	100
I, the Lord of sea and sky	102
I will be with you	104
In the first stage of seeking	116
Jesus, remember me	125
Jesus went away to the desert	127
Let love be real	137
Listen, let your heart keep seeking	142
Lord Jesus Christ	145
Lord of all hopefulness	146
Make me a channel of your peace	152
Never let Jesus	155
Not every day	157
One more step along the world I go	166
Peace is flowing like a river	172
Peace, perfect peace is the gift	173
Praise him in the morning	177
Put your trust	179
Rise and shine	181

Said Judas to Mary	182
Save us, O Lord	183
Seek ye first the kingdom of God	184
Set my heart on fire	185
Step by step, on and on	191
The bell of creation	194
The Spirit lives to set us free	198
The voice from the bush	199
The wise man built his house upon the rock	200
This little light of mine	212
Wait for the Lord	215
We are marching in the light of God	218
With Jesus in the boat	237
Yesterday, today, for ever	238

TAKING RESPONSIBILITY

Do what you know is right	38
Jesus went away to the desert	127
There are people who live in mansions	203
Tick tock	214
We are one family together	219
When God made the garden of creation	228
When your Father made the world	232

REPENTANCE AND FORGIVENESS

Change my heart, O God	29
Enter the darkness	42
God forgave my sin	65
Hear what God says	84
I'm accepted, I'm forgiven	109
Kyrie eleison	134
Lamb of God	135
Lord, have mercy	143
Lord, have mercy on us	144
Lord Jesus Christ	145
Lord, you've promised through your Son	150
O Lamb of God	159
O Lamb of God, you cleanse our hearts	160

THE JOURNEY OF LIFE

Brother, sister, let me serve you	27
Caterpillar, caterpillar	28
Follow me	50
Great indeed are your works	74
In the first stage of seeking	116
Let love be real	137
One more step along the world I go	166
Step by step, on and on	191
The voice from the bush	199
Walk with me, O my Lord	217
We are marching in the light of God	218
With Jesus in the boat	237

PRAYER

A still small voice	3
Abba, Father, send your Spirit	5
All night, all day	8
Anytime, anywhere	18

Be still and know 19
Be still, for the presence of
the Lord 20
Enter the darkness 42
Father, I place into your hands 44
I love to be with you 100
In the first stage of seeking 116
It's me, O Lord 119
Jesus went away to the desert 127
Kum ba yah 133
Listen, let your heart
keep seeking 142
O Lord, hear my prayer 162
Wait for the Lord 215
Waiting for your Spirit 216

MISSION AND EVANGELISM

All of the people 11
All over the world 12
Alleluia, alleluia, give thanks 16
Colours of day 33
Come on, let's get up and go 36
Fishes of the ocean 49
Follow me 50
Go, tell it on the mountain 250
God forgave my sin 65
God our Father gave us life 68
Hang on 77
He gave me eyes so I could see 79
Hear what God says 84
I, the Lord of sea and sky 102
I will be with you 104
Life for the poor was hard
and tough 140
Lord, the light of your love 148
Make me a channel of
your peace 152
O Lord, all the world belongs
to you 161
One hundred and fifty-three! 165
Out to the great wide world
we go 170
Peace is flowing like a river 172
Seek ye first the kingdom
of God 184
The voice from the bush 199
The world is full of smelly feet 201
There's a great big world
out there 206
This little light of mine 212
Tick tock 214
We can plough and dig the land 220
We thank God for the harvest 224
We're going to shine like the sun 226
When your Father made
the world 232

JUSTICE AND PEACE

And everyone beneath the vine
and fig tree 17
Goliath was big and Goliath
was strong 73
He was born in the winter 81
I come like a beggar 95
I'm black, I'm white, I'm short,
I'm tall 110
Life for the poor was hard
and tough 140
Make me a channel of your
peace 152

One hundred and fifty-three! 165
Peace is flowing like a river 172
Peace, perfect peace is the gift 173
Sing praise to God 188
Stand up! Walk tall 190
The voice from the bush 199
There are people who live
in mansions 203
There's a great big world
out there 206
There's a rainbow in the sky 207
We are one family together 219
We're going to shine like the sun 226
When God made the garden
of creation 228
When I needed a neighbour 229
When your Father made
the world 232
Who made the corn grow? 234

FAITH IN THE CITY

A still small voice 3
Colours of day 33
Stand on the corner of the street 189
There are people who live
in mansions 203
We eat the plants that grow
from the seed 221

GOD'S LOVE FOR EVERYBODY

All of the creatures God had
made 10
Boisterous, buzzing,
barking things 25
Clap your hands and sing
this song 32
Colours of day 33
Come on, let's get up and go 36
Enter the darkness 42
Friends, all gather here in a circle 51
Go wandering in the sun 63
God turned darkness into light 70
He's got the whole world in
his hand 82
Hear what God says 84
I, the Lord of sea and sky 102
I'm black, I'm white, I'm short,
I'm tall 110
Jesus had all kind of friends 121
Jesus' love is very wonderful 123
Life for the poor was hard
and tough 140
Nobody's a nobody 156
Over the earth is a mat of green 171
Sing praise to God 188
Stand up! Walk tall 190
The King is among us 197
There are hundreds of sparrows 202
There are people who live
in mansions 203
There's a great big world
out there 206
There's a seed 208
Think big: an elephant 209
Tick tock 214
We thank God for the harvest 224
When God made the garden
of creation 228
Whether you're one 233
Zip bam boo 244

VALUING EACH OTHER

A new commandment 1
All of the creatures God
had made 1
Bind us together, Lord 2
Boisterous, buzzing,
barking things 2
Brother, sister, let me serve you 2
Father, I place into your hands 4
Friends, all gather here in a
circle 5
From heaven you came 5
God forgave my sin 6
God our Father gave us life 6
I come like a beggar 9
I'm black, I'm white, I'm short,
I'm tall 11
In the upper room 11
Isn't it good 11
Jesus had all kinds of friends 12
Jesus put this song into
our hearts 12
Just imagine 13
Let love be real 13
Love is like a circle 15
One hundred and fifty-three! 16
Said Judas to Mary 18
Sing praise to God 18
The world is full of smelly feet 20
There are people who live
in mansions 20
Think of a world without
any flowers 21
We're going to shine like
the sun 22
When God made the garden
of creation 22
When I needed a neighbour 22

REDEMPTION AND SALVATION

Colours of day 33
Do not be afraid 3
Father welcomes all his children 4
Follow me 50
From heaven you came 52
Give thanks with a grateful
heart 57
He was born in the winter 81
How did Moses cross the
Red Sea? 92
I danced in the morning 96
I, the Lord of sea and sky 102
Jesus is greater 122
Lord Jesus Christ 145
O Lamb of God 159
O Lamb of God, you cleanse
our hearts 160
O when the saint go
marching in 163
Sing glory to God 187
Sing lullaby 263
The Spirit lives to set us free 198
The voice from the bush 199
There is a green hill 204
There's a rainbow in the sky 207
Wait for the Lord 215
What kind of man was this 227
With Jesus in the boat 237
Zacchaeus was a very little man 243
Zip bam boo 244

THE KINGSHIP OF CHRIST

Alleluia, alleluia, give thanks 16
Born in the night 246
Come into his presence 34
Come on and celebrate 35
Each of us is a living stone 41
From heaven you came 52
Give me joy in my heart 55
Gloria 58
Glory and honour to God
in the highest 59
Glory, glory in the highest 60
Glory to God 61
Glory to God, to God in
the height 62
He is the King 80
Holy, holy, holy is the Lord 88
Holy, most holy (Skye Boat Song) 89
Holy, most holy (Slane) 90
Hosanna, hosanna, hosanna
in the highest 91
Jesus is greater 122
Jesus, remember me 125
Jesus will never, ever 128
Joy to the world 254
King of kings 132
Lord, the light of your love 148
Said Judas to Mary 182
Sing glory to God 187
We have a King who rides
a donkey 222
Who's the king of the jungle? 236
You are the King of glory 239
Zip bam boo 244

THE CHURCH'S YEAR

ADVENT

All of the people 11
And everyone beneath the vine
and fig tree 17
I come like a beggar 95
I, the Lord of sea and sky 102
Kum ba yah 133
Never let Jesus 155
Wait for the Lord 215
The angel Gabriel from
heaven came 264

CHRISTMAS

Away in a manger 245
Be still, for the presence of
the Lord 20
Born in the night 246
Come and join the celebration 247
Come into his presence 34
Come, they told me 248
Everyone's a Christmas baby 249
Go, tell it on the mountain 250
God was born on earth 251
Hee haw! Hee haw! 252
I wonder as I wander 253
Joy to the world 254
Light a flame 255
Lord Jesus Christ 145
Mary had a baby 256
Mary said to Joseph 257
O come, all ye faithful 258

O little town of Bethlehem 259
Once in royal David's city 260
See him lying on a bed
of straw 261
Silent night 262
Sing lullaby 263
The angel Gabriel from
heaven came 264
The first nowell 265
The holly and the ivy 266
There's a star in the east 267
We three kings of Orient are 268
We wish you a merry Christmas 269
While shepherds watched 270

EPIPHANY

Be still, for the presence of
the Lord 20
Great indeed are your works 74
Holy, most holy (Skye Boat Song) 89
Holy, most holy (Slane) 90
Joy to the world 254
Lord, the light of your love 148
We three kings of Orient are 268

LENT

Change my heart, O God 29
Do what you know is right 38
Enter the darkness 42
Follow me 50
From heaven you cane 52
God forgave my sin 65
Jesus, remember me 125
Jesus went away to the desert 127
Kyrie eleison 134
Lamb of God 135
Lord, have mercy 143
Lord, have mercy on us 144
Lord, you've promised
through your Son 150
O Lamb of God 159
O Lamb of God, you cleanse
our hearts 160

PALM SUNDAY

Clap your hands, all you people 31
Give me joy in my heart 55
Ho, ho, ho, hosanna 86
Hosanna, hosanna, hosanna
in the highest 91
We have a King who rides
a donkey 222

PASSIONTIDE

From heaven you came 52
In the upper room 117
Jesus, remember me 125
There is a green hill 204
What kind of man was this 227

EASTER

A butterfly, an Easter egg 1
All in an Easter garden 7
Alleluia, alleluia, give thanks 16
72, Morning has broken 153
We have a King who rides
a donkey 222

PENTECOST

Abba, Father, send your Spirit 5
All over the world 12
Hang on 77
Listen, let your heart keep
seeking 142
Waiting for your Spirit 216
When the Spirit of the Lord 231
You've got to move 242

HARVEST

God almighty set a rainbow 64
Laudato sii 136
Push, little seed 178
Thank you, Lord 193
We can plough and dig the land 220
We eat the plants that grow
from the seed 221
We plough the fields,
and scatter 223
We thank God for the harvest 224
Who made the corn grow? 234

REMEMBRANCE SUNDAY

And everyone beneath the vine
and fig tree 17
God sends a rainbow 69
I'm black, I'm white, I'm short,
I'm tall 110
Make me a channel of your
peace 152
One more step along the world
I go 166
Peace is flowing like a river 172
Peace, perfect peace is the gift 173

WORSHIP

MORNING

Give thanks to the Lord 56
God turned darkness into light 70
Morning has broken 153
The clock tells the story of time 195
This is the day 211

EVENING

All night, all day 8
Save us, O Lord 183

BAPTISM/CONFIRMATION

Abba, Father, send your Spirit 5
All over the world 12
Be the centre of my life 21
Change my heart, O God 29
Do what you know is right 38
Don't build your house on
the sandy land 40
Every minute of every day 43
Father, I place into your hands 44
Father welcomes all his children 48
Follow me 50
Give me joy in my heart 55
Hang on 77
Have you heard the raindrops 78
He's got the whole world in
his hand 82

He's the same today 83
I, the Lord of sea and sky 102
I will click my fingers 105
I'm accepted, I'm forgiven 109
In the first stage of seeking 116
Listen, let your heart keep
seeking 142
Make me a channel of your
peace 152
My mouth was made for
worship 154
Never let Jesus 155
O when the saint go marching in 163
One more step along the world
I go 166
Set my heart on fire 185
Step by step, on and on 191
The wise man built his house
upon the rock 200
There are hundreds of sparrows 202
Tick tock 214
Waiting for your Spirit 216

OPENING OF WORSHIP

All creatures of our God and King 6
Be still, for the presence of
the Lord 20
Come into his presence 34
Come on and celebrate 35
Friends, all gather here in a
circle 51
Hey, now, everybody sing 85
I was so glad 103
I will enter his gates 106
I will sing, I will sing 107
Isn't it good 118
Jubilate, everybody 130
Lord, the light of your love 148
Lord, we've come to worship you 149
Morning has broken 153
Praise and thanksgiving 174
Praise God in his holy place 176
The King is among us 197
This is the day 211
You've got to move 242

PRAISE AND THANKSGIVING

A butterfly, an Easter egg 1
All creatures of our God and King 6
All of my heart 9
All the nations of the earth 14
Alleluia, alleluia, give thanks 16
Bless the Lord, O my soul 23
'Cheep!' said the sparrow 30
Clap your hands, all you people 31
Come into his presence 34
Come on and celebrate 35
Come on, let's get up and go 36
Do you ever wish you could fly 39
Father, we want to thank you 47
Fishes of the ocean 49
From my knees to my nose 53

Give me joy in my heart 55
Give thanks to the Lord 56
Give thanks with a grateful
heart 57
Glory and honour to God in the
highest 59
Glory, glory in the highest 60
Glory to God 61
Glory to God 62
God's not 72
Great indeed are your works 74
Halle, halle, halle 75
Hallelu, hallelu 76
He is the King 80
He's got the whole world in
his hand 82
Hey, now, everybody sing 85
Ho, ho, ho, hosanna 86
Holy, most holy (Skye Boat Song) 89
Holy, most holy (Slane) 90
I feel spring in the air today 97
I reach up high 101
I was so glad 103
I will sing, I will sing 107
I will wave my hands 108
I'm gonna click 112
I've got peace like a river 113
If I were a butterfly 114
If I were an astronaut 115
Jesus' love is very wonderful 123
Jesus put this song into
our hearts 124
Jubilate, everybody 130
King of kings 132
Laudato sii 136
Let the mountains dance
and sing 138
Lord, we've come to worship you 149
Morning has broken 153
My mouth was made for
worship 154
O give thanks 158
Oh! Oh! Oh! how good is
the Lord 164
Our God is so great 169
Praise and thanksgiving 174
Praise God from whom all
blessings flow 175
Praise God in his holy place 176
Praise him in the morning 177
Rise and shine 181
Sing glory to God 187
Thank you for the summer
morning 192
Thank you, Lord 193
There was one, there were two 205
Think big: an elephant 209
Think of a world without
any flowers 210
We will praise 225
When the Spirit of the Lord 231
Yesterday, today, for ever 238
You are the King of glory 239

HOLY COMMUNION

A butterfly, an Easter egg 1
Abba, Father, let me be 4
Be still and know 19
Be still, for the presence of
the Lord 20
Bind us together, Lord 22
Blest are you, Lord, God of
all creation 24
Break the bread and pour
the wine 26
Brother, sister, let me serve you 27
Enter the darkness 42
Gather around for the table
is spread 54
Gloria 58
Glory and honour to God in
the highest 59
Glory, glory in the highest 60
Glory to God 61
Glory to God, to God in
the height 62
God forgave my sin 65
Holy, holy, holy is the Lord 88
Holy, most holy (Skye Boat Song) 89
Holy, most holy (Slane) 90
I come like a beggar 95
In the upper room 117
Jesus calls us to a party 120
Jesus took a piece of bread 126
Kyrie eleison 134
Lamb of God 135
Let love be real 137
Let us talents and tongues
employ 139
Life for the poor was hard and
tough 140
Lord, have mercy 143
Lord, have mercy on us 144
Lord Jesus Christ 145
Lord, the light of your love 148
O Lamb of God 159
O Lamb of God, you cleanse
our hearts 160
Sing glory to God 187

OFFERTORY

Abba, Father, let me be 4
All that I am 13
Come on and celebrate 35

CLOSE OF WORSHIP

Come on, let's get up and go 36
Holy God 87
I will be with you 104
Out to the great wide world
we go 170
There's a great big world
out there 206
You shall go out with joy 241

Stories and Characters from the Bible

MIRACLES OF JESUS

Calming the wind and the sea
Walk with me, O my Lord 217
With Jesus in the boat 237

Healing of the woman bent double in the Synagogue
Stand up! Walk tall 190

Healing the blind
Walk with me, O my Lord 217

Miraculous catch of fish
One hundred and fifty-three! 165

Walking on the sea
Walk with me, O my Lord 217

Walking on water
I will be with you 104

Water into wine
Life for the poor was hard and tough 140
What kind of man was this 227

PARABLES OF JESUS

Dives and Lazarus
There are people who live in mansions 203

House built on sand
Don't build your house on the sandy land 40
The wise man built his house upon the rock 200

Last Judgement
When I needed a neighbour 229

Lost Sheep
I have a friend 99

Sheep and goats
When I needed a neighbour 229

Sower
We thank God for the harvest 224

Wise and foolish bridesmaids
Give me joy in my heart 55

BIBLICAL CHARACTERS

Angel at the tomb
All in an Easter garden 7

Angels at the Nativity
I wonder as a I wander 253
Light a flame 255
O come, all ye faithful 258
O little town of Bethlehem 259
See him lying on a bed of straw 261
Silent night 262
Sing lullaby 263
The first nowell 265
There's a start in the east 267
While shepherds watched 270

Archangel Gabriel
The angel Gabriel from heaven came 264

David
I was so glad 103
When the Spirit of the Lord 231

David and Goliath
Goliath was big and Goliath was strong 73

James and John
I danced in the morning 96

Joseph, husband of Mary
Hee haw! Hee haw! 252
Mary said to Joseph 257

Judas Iscariot
Said Judas to Mary 182

Mary, mother of Jesus
Everyone's a Christmas baby 249
I wonder as I wander 253
Mary had a baby 256
Mary said to Joseph 257
O little town of Bethlehem 259
Once in royal David's city 260
See him lying on a bed of straw 261
Silent night 262

The angel Gabriel from heaven came 264
The holly and ivy 266

Mary of Bethany
Said Judas to Mary 182

Moses
How did Moses cross the Red Sea? 92
The voice from the bush 199

Noah
All of the creatures God had made 10
Rise and shine 181
There's a rainbow in the sky 207

Peter
In the upper room 117

Scribes and Pharisees
I danced in the morning 96

Shepherds at the Nativity
Come and join the celebration 247
Go, tell it on the mountain 250
God was born on earth 251
I wonder as I wander 253
O come, all ye faithful 258
See him lying on a bed of straw 261
Silent night 262
The first nowell 65
There's a star in the east 267
While shepherds watched 270

Wise Men
Come and join the celebration 247
I wonder as I wander 253
O come, all ye faithful 258
The first nowell 265
We three kings of Orient are 268

Woman bent double in the synagogue
Stand up! Walk tall 190

Women at the tomb
All in an Easter garden 7

Zacchaeus
Zacchaeus was a very little man 243

Scriptural Index

GENESIS
1   25, 49, 70, 153, 228, 232
2   228
6:13-8:18   181
7   10
9:13   64, 69, 207

EXODUS
3:1-10   20, 199
14:21-22   92

NUMBERS
6:24-26   87

1 SAMUEL
17:4-50   73

2 SAMUEL
6:14   231

1 KINGS
19:12   3

PSALMS
23:4   217
24:1   161
27:14   215
33:3   107
46:10   19
47:1   29
95:1-2   130
96:1   107
98:1   107
100   130
103:1   23
108:1   107
118   211, 41
121   103
126:5-6   107
136:1   158
139:1   148
144:9   107
148   49, 136
149:1   107
150   225

ISAIAH
6   102
7:14   145
13:6   215
29:16   29
40:3-5   215
42:10   107
42:23   138
43:1-4   37
45:9   29
49:13   138
55:12   241
64:8   29

JEREMIAH
18:6   29
31:3   84

MICAH
4:3   17

HABAKKUK
2:14   12

MATTHEW
2:1-12   247,253, 259, 261, 265
3:13-17   48
4:1-10   127, 184
4:18-22   50
4:19   191
5:14   255
5:16   212
5:44   161
6:9-13   167, 168
6:28-29   202
6:33   184
6:34   191
7:7   184
7:24-27   40, 200
8:18-22   50, 191
8:23-27   179, 237
9:9   50, 191
10:8   65
10:29-31   30, 202
10:34-39   50
14:13-21   54
14:22-33   104, 179, 237
15:32-38   54
16:24-25   50
18:20   51, 107, 118
19:14   48
19:21   50
20:25-28   27, 52, 161
21:1-11   31, 91, 222
21:42   41
22:37-40   185
25:1-13   55
25:31-46   182, 229
26:26-27   54, 126
26:31-32   50
26:39   52
28:1-7   7
28:18-20   38, 65, 104

MARK
1:9-11   48
1:12-13   127
1:16-20   50
1:17   191
2:14   50, 191
4:35-41   217, 237
6:34-44   54
6:45-52   179, 237
7:7   5
8:1-10   54
8:34   50
10:14   48
10:42-45   27, 52, 161
11:1-10   222
11:9   31, 91
12:10   41
12:30-31   185
14:22   54
14:22-23   126
14:27-28   50
14:36   52
16:1-6   7

LUKE
1:26-38   264
1:46   264
2:4-7   260
2:7   245, 252, 253, 256, 257, 261
2:8-20   250, 251, 253, 261, 262, 265, 267, 270
2:9-14   259
2:10   255
2:13-14   258
2:15-20   247
3:21-22   48
4:1-12   127, 184
5:11   50
5:27   191
6:27   161
6:35   161
6:47-49   40, 200
8:22-25   237
9:11-17   54
10:7   185
11:1   145
11:2-4   167, 168
11:9   5
12:6-7   30, 202
12:27-28   202
13:10-17   190
15:3-7   99
16:19-31   203
18:16   48
19:1-5   243
19:37-38   31, 91
20:17   41
22:19-20   54,126, 145
22:42   52
23:42   125
24:30-31   54
24:49   77

JOHN
1:29   135, 159, 160
1:36   135, 159, 160
1:43   191
4:10-15   78, 240
6:5-13   54
6:16-21   179, 237
6:68   239
7:37-38   78, 240
8:12   33, 148
8:32   148
8:36   107
10:27   191
12:1-8   182
12:13   31, 91
12:14-15   222
12:26   191
13:1-15   201
13:5-14   117
13:34-35   2
14:6   122, 191
14:16-18   50, 198
15:19   161
2:1-11   140, 227
21:4-11   165
21:15-17   104

ACTS
2:1-18   77
4:11   41
17:6   161

ROMANS
8:15   5
9:21   29
15:3-4   145

1 CORINTHIANS
3:6   220
7:5   107
11:18   107
11:23-25 54, 126, 145
11:33   107
14:26   107

2 CORINTHIANS
3:17-18   148

GALATIANS
4:6   5

EPHESIANS
3:18   71, 123

PHILIPPIANS
4:4   180

HEBREWS
10:19   148
13:8   83, 128, 238

1 PETER
2:4-7   41

1 JOHN
2:8   33

REVELATION
4:8   88
7:17   78, 240
21:5   161
21:6   78, 240
22:1   78, 240
22:17   78, 240

Index of First Lines

This index gives the first line of each hymn. If a hymn is known also
by a title (e.g. *Shine, Jesus, Shine*) this is indicated in italics.

A

A butterfly, an Easter egg	1
A new commandment	2
A still small voice	3
Abba, Father, let me be	4
Abba, Father, send your Spirit	5
Ain't listenin' to no temptation	127
All creatures of our God and King	6
All in an Easter garden	7
All night, all day	8
All of my heart	9
All of the creatures God had made	10
All of the people	11
All over the world	12
All that I am	13
All the nations of the earth	14
All things bright and beautiful	15
Alleluia, alleluia, give thanks to the risen Lord	16
And everyone beneath the vine and fig tree	17
Anytime, anywhere	18
Away in a manger	245

B

Be still and know	19
Be still, for the presence of the Lord	20
Be the centre of my life	21
Beautiful world	213
Big and little you's and me's	25
Biggest isn't always best	73
Bind us together, Lord	22
Bless the Lord, O my soul	23
Blest are you, Lord, God of all creation	24
Boisterous, buzzing, barking things	25
Born in the night	246
Break the bread and pour the wine	26
Brother, sister, let me serve you	27

C

Calypso Carol	261
Care for your world	232
Caribbean Lord's Prayer	167
Caterpillar, caterpillar	28
Celebrate	35
Change my heart, O God	29
'Cheep!' said the sparrow	30
Circle of friends	51
Clap, clap Gloria	58
Clap your hands, all you people	31
Clap your hands and sing this song	32
Colours of day	33
Colours of hope	69
Come and join the celebration	247
Come into his presence	34
Come on and celebrate	35
Come on, let's get up and go	36
Come, they told me	248
Country Gardens Gloria	62

D

Deeper, wider, higher	71
Do not be afraid	37
Do what you know is right	38
Do you ever wish you could fly	39
Don't build your house on the sandy land	40
Doxology	175

E

Each of us is a living stone	41
Early one morning Gloria	59
Enter the darkness	42
Every minute of every day	43
Everyone's a Christmas baby	249

F

Father, I place into your hands	44
Father, we adore you	45
Father, we love you	46
Father, we want to thank you	47
Father welcomes all his children	48
Fishes of the ocean	49
Follow me	50
Freely, freely	65
Friends, all gather here in a circle	51
From heaven you came	52
From my knees to my nose	53

G

Gather around for the table is spread	54
Give me joy in my heart	55
Give thanks to the Lord	56
Give thanks with a grateful heart	57
Gloria	58
Glorify your name	46
Glory and honour to God in the highest	59
Glory, glory in the highest	60
Glory to God	61
Glory to God, to God in the height	62
Go, tell it on the mountain	250
Go wandering in the sun	63
God almighty set a rainbow	64
God forgave my sin	65
God has spoken	66
God is living everywhere	189
God is the centre and the circle	67
God knows me	202
God our Father gave us life	68
God sends a rainbow	69
God turned darkness into light	70
God was born on earth	251
God's love is deeper	71
God's not dead	72
Goliath was big and Goliath was strong	73
Gotta get out and scatter some seed	224
Gotta put the world to rights	203
Great indeed are your works	74

H

Halle, halle, halle	75
Hallelu, hallelu	76
Hang on	77
Have you heard the raindrops	78
He gave me eyes so I could see	79
He has made me glad	106
He is the King	80
He made me	79
He was born in the winter	81
He's got the whole world in his hand	82
He's the same today	83
Hear what God says	84
Hee haw! Hee haw!	252
Here I am, Lord	102
Hey, now, everybody sing	85
Ho, ho, ho, hosanna	86
Holy God	87
Holy, holy, holy is the Lord	88
Holy, most holy, all holy the Lord (Skye Boat Song)	89
Holy, most holy, all holy the Lord (Slane)	90
Hosanna, hosanna, hosanna in the highest	91
Hosanna to the Son of David	239
How did Moses cross the Red Sea?	92
How great is our God	93

I

I am cold, I am ice	94
I come like a beggar	95
I danced in the morning	96
I feel spring in the air today	97
I gotta home in gloryland	98
I have a friend	99
I have loved you	84
I love to be with you	100
I reach up high	101
I, the Lord of sea and sky	102
I was so glad	103
I will be with you	104
I will click my fingers	105
I will enter his gates	106
I will sing, I will sing	107
I will wave my hands	108
I wonder as I wander	253
I'm accepted, I'm forgiven	109
I'm black, I'm white, I'm short, I'm tall	110
I'm glad I'm alive	111
I'm gonna click	112
I've got peace like a river	113
If I were a butterfly	114
If I were an astronaut	115
In the first stage of seeking	116
In the upper room	117
Isn't it good	118
It's me, O Lord	119

J

Jesus calls us to a party	120
Jesus had all kinds of friends	121

Jesus is greater 122
Jesus is the living way 191
Jesus' love is very wonderful 123
Jesus put this song
into our hearts 124
Jesus, remember me 125
Jesus took a piece of bread 126
*Jesus turned the water
into wine* 140
Jesus went away to the desert 127
Jesus will never, ever 128
Jesus, you love me 129
Joy to the world 254
Jubilate, everybody 130
Judas and Mary 182
*Just be glad God made
you 'you'* 39
*Just a little bit of bread
and a little bit of wine* 120
Just imagine 131

K

King of kings 132
Kum ba yah 133
Kyrie 144
Kyrie eleison 134

L

Lamb of God 135
Laudato sii 136
Lead my people to freedom 199
Let love be real 137
Let the mountains dance and sing 138
Let us talents and tongues
employ 139
Life for the poor was hard
and tough 140
Life is for living now 141
Light a flame 255
Light up the fire 33
Listen, let your heart
keep seeking 142
Living Lord 145
Living stones 41
Lord, forgive us 150
Lord, have mercy 143
Lord, have mercy on us 144
Lord Jesus Christ 145
Lord of all hopefulness 146
Lord of the Dance 96
Lord of the future 147
Lord, the light of your love 148
Lord, we've come to
worship you 149
Lord, you've promised through
your Son 150
Love is like a circle 151

M

Make me a channel of
your peace 152
Mary had a baby 256
Mary said to Joseph 257
Morning has broken 153
My best friend 18
My mouth was made for worship 154

N

Never let Jesus 155
*Never mind the sheep,
look for the baby* 251

No one will ever be the same 226
Nobody's a nobody 156
Not every day 157

O

O come, all ye faithful 258
O give thanks 158
O Lamb of God 159
O Lamb of God, you cleanse
our hearts 160
O little town of Bethlehem 259
O Lord, all the world belongs
to you 161
O Lord, hear my prayer 162
O when the saints go
marching in 163
Oh! Oh! Oh! how good
is the Lord 164
Once in royal David's city 260
One hundred and fifty-three! 165
One more step along the
world I go 166
Our Father (Caribbean) 167
Our Father (Wiener) 168
Our God is so great 169
Out to the great wide
world we go 170
Over the earth is a mat of green 171

P

Peace is flowing like a river 172
Peace, perfect peace is the gift 173
Peruvian Gloria 61
Praise and thanksgiving 174
Praise God from whom all
blessings flow 175
Praise God in his holy place 176
Praise him in the morning 177
Push, little seed 178
Put your trust 179

R

Rejoice in the Lord always 180
Right where you are 193
Rise and shine 181
Rise up, shepherd, and follow 267

S

Said Judas to Mary 182
Sandy Land 40
Save us, O Lord 183
See him lying on a bed of straw 261
Seek ye first the kingdom of God 184
Set my heart on fire 185
*Seven stages of spiritual
growth* 116
Shalom, my friend 186
Shine, Jesus, shine 148
Signs of new life 1
Silent night 262
Sing glory to God 187
Sing hosanna 55
Sing lullaby 263
Sing praise to God 188
Skye Sanctus 89
Slane Sanctus 90
Spring in the air 97
Stand on the corner of the street 189
Stand up! Walk tall 190
Standing in the need of prayer 119
Step by step, on and on 191

T

Thank you for the summer
morning 192
Thank you, Lord 193
The angel Gabriel from
heaven came 264
The Ash Grove Gloria 187
The bell of creation 194
The birds' song 30
The children's band 205
The clock tells the story of time 195
The donkey's Christmas carol 252
The duck goes 'Quack' 196
The first nowell 265
The holly and the ivy 266
The King is among us 197
The little drummer boy 248
The Servant King 52
The Spirit lives to set us free 198
The trees of the field 241
The vine and fig tree 17
The voice from the bush 199
The wise man built his house
upon the rock 200
The world is full of smelly feet 201
There are hundreds of sparrows 202
There are people who live
in mansions 203
There is a green hill 204
There was one, there were two 205
There wasn't any room
at the inn 257
There's a great big world
out there 206
There's a rainbow in the sky 207
There's a seed 208
There's a star in the east 267
Think big: an elephant 209
Think of a world without
any flowers 210
This is the day 211
This little light of mine 212
This world you have made 213
Tick tock 214
To be with you 100

W

Wait for the Lord 215
Waiting for your Spirit 216
Walk in the light 198
Walk with me, O my Lord 217
Water 240
Water of life 78
We are marching in the
light of God 218
We are one family together 219
We can plough and dig the land 220
We eat the plants that grow
from the seed 221
We have a King who rides
a donkey 222
We plough the fields,
and scatter 223
We thank God for the harvest 224
We three kings of Orient are 268
We will praise 225
We wish you a merry
Christmas 269
We're going to shine
like the sun 226
What kind of man was this 227

When God made the garden
  of creation 228
When I needed a neighbour 229
When Jesus was my age 230
When the Spirit of the Lord 231
When your Father made
  the world 232
Whether you're one 233
While shepherds watched 270

Who made the corn grow? 234
Who put the colours in
  the rainbow? 235
Who's the king of the jungle? 236
With Jesus in the boat 237

Y

Yesterday, today, for ever 238
You are the King of glory 239

You can drink it, swim in it 240
You must do for others 117
You shall go out with joy 241
You've got to move 242

Z

Zacchaeus was a very
  little man 243
Zip bam boo 244